SURVIVING SICKLE CELL

WHILE TRYING TO LIVE REGULAR

KALYSIA JOHNSON

authorHOUSE®

AuthorHouse™
1663 Liberty Drive
Bloomington, IN 47403
www.authorhouse.com
Phone: 833-262-8899

Published by AuthorHouse 11/11/2022

ISBN: 978-1-6655-0407-2 (sc)
ISBN: 978-1-6655-0408-9 (hc)
ISBN: 978-1-6655-0409-6 (e)

Library of Congress Control Number: 2020920202

Print information available on the last page.

Any people depicted in stock imagery provided by Getty Images are models, and such images are being used for illustrative purposes only. Certain stock imagery © Getty Images.

This book is printed on acid-free paper.

Because of the dynamic nature of the Internet, any web addresses or links contained in this book may have changed since publication and may no longer be valid. The views expressed in this work are solely those of the author and do not necessarily reflect the views of the publisher, and the publisher hereby disclaims any responsibility for them.

This book is dedicated to everyone with sickle cell anemia and the sickle cell trait. I wrote the book to encourage, motivate, and inspire anyone with this life-threatening disease. I am a living testimony that you can live a normal and semi-regular life with sickle cell anemia.

IN LOVING MEMORY OF
KALYSIA JOHNSON

It is with a shattered and heavy heart that I must write this tribute. During the early morning of August 1, 2020, Kalysia woke up in severe and unbearable pain. She was in a total body crisis, which attacked all of her extremities as well as her chest. Kalysia was taken to the hospital by her husband and son. They were not allowed to remain with her, as usual, because of the hospitals strict COVID-19 regulations. Kalysia desperately feared going to the hospital during the pandemic because she did not want to put herself into harm's way. Nevertheless, she did not have a choice in the matter because the magnitude of her pain was beyond insufferable. Moreover, she was well aware that any time she had a chest crisis it was mandatory protocol for her to go directly to the hospital. She never wavered in doing so, because she knew that chest crises were extremely dangerous. Kalysia was conscious of the fact that they could cause acute chest syndrome (ACS), which is the leading cause of death for patients with sickle cell disease (SCD).

Thank God for the advancements in technology because my family and I were able to communicate with Kalysia every day by phone, text message or FaceTime. She described this episode as the absolute worst crisis that she had ever experienced in her lifetime. Kalysia was unable to find the slightest bit of comfort or relief, despite the fact that she was being heavily medicated with some of the most potent known pain medications available. She labored in this state for the entire duration of her six day admittance. We last spoke to her at approximately 1:30 p.m. on August 6, 2020. Kalysia was very upset because the doctors were speaking negatively about her condition. In short, they informed her that she would possibly be bedridden, because she was unable to walk independently anymore. We are a religious family; therefore, we went into prayer mode. We instantaneously started feeding her words of encouragement and reminded her God can do all things but fail. We reassured her that God had the final say, and He was the Great Physician!

Our conversation ended with exchanges of "I love you." We wanted to allow her some time to rest and had plans to FaceTime her a few hours later. However, before we had an opportunity to do so, I received a devastating call from her husband. He told me that Kalysia had gone into cardiac arrest, and the doctors were vigorously performing CPR on her. Without pause, I began fervently praying at the top of my lungs and bartering with God for my sister's life! I recited every healing Scripture that I knew and reminded God of His promises. I begged Kalysia to continue to fight and not leave us. Sadly, my desperate pleas and prayers were not answered. Even still, I undoubtedly know that she fought for her life until she took her very last breath, because she was a warrior! Likewise, Kalysia wanted nothing more than to have longevity of life, because she did not want to prematurely leave her family behind, especially her beloved son. Kalysia willed him into this world, and she fiercely loved him from the depths of her soul! He was her greatest accomplishment, and she only placed him second to God.

Kalysia was my dearly loved sissy, BFF and my One! She was born with Sickle Cell, and Kalysia tirelessly battled with the disease for forty-seven years. At times, the hospital was like a second home to her, which caused Kalysia to spend many birthdays and holidays in-patient. My sister endured countless debilitating crises throughout her lifetime, which resulted in her being forced to suffer tumultuous pain. Not even morphine or the strongest of opioids were able to relieve her insurmountable and excruciating pain. Kalysia received numerous blood transfusions, yet they only provided her with temporary relief for her chronic illness. She truly endured more than her fair share of challenging and turbulent times. Even still, Kalysia remained encouraged and hopeful!

She fought the good fight of faith and always counted her blessings. Kalysia never allowed sickle cell to define who she was or what she could accomplish in her life. She never felt sorry for herself or allowed anyone else to do so. Despite her disease, Kalysia considered herself to be abundantly blessed and lived her life to the fullest and never took it for granted! Her relentless spirit, strong will and determination fueled Kalysia's warrior mentality. Moreover, these desirable traits enabled her to achieve every goal that she set for herself—especially her higher learning endeavors and desires to become a published author. Before Kalysia's untimely demise, she had just finished writing her fourth novel.

Kalysia earned her post-graduate degree in Psychology and was actively pursuing her doctoral degree in Psychology. Kalysia was extremely intelligent and had a passion for learning. She had a brilliant mind with limitless potential! She was also a reliable, dedicated and hard-working educator for more than 30 years. Kalysia prided herself on being able to help shape and foster the minds of young children during their most fundamental years of growth! She was also a pillar in her church community, where she served in a leadership role as one of the first ladies, a Sunday school teacher, and an invaluable member of the hospitality committee. Kalysia also wrote and directed all of the plays and speeches for the youth department. She was a phenomenal woman and a beautiful person both inside and out.

Kalysia was generous, kindhearted, and had an infectious smile. She was a social butterfly and people gravitated toward her because she had a magnetic personality! Kalysia never met a stranger and always rooted for the underdog. She was a selfless and free spirited person! Kalysia was very compassionate and never bypassed an opportunity to lend a helping hand to someone in need. She would give you the shirt off of her back. Kalysia was happiest whenever she was able to make a deposit into someone else's life. She had an optimistic outlook and always aimed high. Kalysia was extremely driven, ambitious, motivated, determined, and outgoing. She was a true Fashionista, from the top of her head to the soles of her feet. Kalysia was also an avid reader. Additionally, she loved to travel, shop, and experience new things.

Kalysia was a total mama's girl! Anytime I answered the phone before our mom did, she would affectionately say, "Hey, Lay, where's my mama? I need to talk to her." Yes, as if she were an only child (smile). She was the last one of the daughters to leave home, and Kalysia didn't move very far away from our mom at all. Instead, she moved directly upstairs from her favorite girl—her mama! It was a sensible decision for more than just healthcare reasons, because they had a close knit, beautiful relationship. During Kalysia's young adulthood, they spent time together every day. They frequently dined at one of their favorite restaurants and went shopping together on a regular basis. As time went on, Kalysia was blessed to start her own family. In doing so, she made sure to weave her mama into the fabric of her immediate family. Their relationship did not skip a beat! If anything, it became even stronger because our mother played a very pivotal role in her grandson's upbringing. She was a SUPER nanny to him! Kalysia already knew that would be the case, and I'm sure that's one of the reasons why she named him after her— Jayce for Joyce. The last decade of Kalysia's life was an extremely busy time period for her. She was tirelessly juggling being a devoted wife and mother, an exceptional teacher, and a stellar student. Nevertheless, she made a concerted effort to maintain her closeness with her mama. Kalysia continued to call her every day, take her to all of her appointments, run errands for and with her as well as taking her out to eat. She treated every day as a special occasion, where her mama was concerned!

She was a loving, loyal and devoted daughter, wife, mother, sister, aunt, great-aunt, cousin, friend, educator, and co-worker. Anyone that ever knew her, crossed paths with her, or merely brushed up against her should consider themselves blessed... for you were touched by an Angel! Although Kalysia has transitioned on to be with the Lord, we are confident that not only is she resting peacefully, but also we shall see her again. Moreover, she is pain-free and completely healed of the monster that is known as sickle cell disease! Kalysia's sudden and unexpected departure has left an immeasurable hole in our hearts. We will mourn her until we join her!

Earlasha "Lasha" Williams (#MySister'sKeeper), one of Kalysia's loving siblings

About Sickle Cell Disease (SCD)

Sickle Cell Disease is a genetic red blood cell disorder that is present at birth. It is inherited when a child receives two sickle cell genes—one from each parent. Healthy red blood cells are round, like discs. They move through small blood vessels to carry oxygen to all parts of the body. In someone who has SCD, the red blood cells become hard and sticky and look like a C-shape or crescent moon. The sickle cells die early, which causes a constant shortage of red blood cells. Also, when they travel through small blood vessels, they get stuck and clog the blood flow. The sickle-shaped cells can also stick to the vessel walls. When this happens, oxygen can't reach nearby tissues. The lack of oxygen can cause sudden attacks of catastrophic pain, called pain crises. These attacks can occur without warning! This chronic, grave condition can trigger other serious problems such as infection, acute chest syndrome, organ damage, and stroke. Conclusively, SCD disproportionately affects people of African descent more than any other race, by roughly 90%. Nevertheless, reports show that Hispanics, Asians and Caucasians are also susceptible to getting SCD!

https://www.cdc.gov/ncbddd/sicklecell/facts.html

PREFACE

When I was younger, I was given a booklet that was about thirty pages long. It was about sickle cell anemia. I have had that book for almost forty-two years, and it was my guide to having sickle cell as well as how to manage the disease. I must have read that book a million times.

I decided to write my own book because I have a personal story to share and want to inspire everyone, children and adults, who ever wanted to know about sickle cell anemia. I personally feel my disease does not get the proper recognition it deserves.

Sickle cell is a serious disease that is life-threatening and can be exceedingly difficult to live with at times. I have some good days as well as some bad days. I try to live with sickle cell anemia while trying to live a regular and somewhat normal life. Having sickle cell is difficult because of how painful it is, but it has been both a blessing and a curse at the same time. The curse has been in being sick all my life, and the blessing is the fact that I was born with sickle cell anemia and not something worse.

I want to share my story because I am surviving sickle cell every day. I live my life as if I do not have the disease. My mother always treated me the same way she treated my siblings; I did not get treated any differently. However, when I was sick and was in a crisis, I did receive special treatment.

Sickle cell anemia is a blood disorder that is hereditary. The blood cells of people who have sickle cell are not circular like those of people who don't have sickle cell. Instead, their blood cells are shaped like sickles, and that is why the disease is called sickle cell.

People who have sickle cell might experience breathing issues, extreme tiredness, and dizziness as well as mild or severe headaches from time to time. They may also experience weakness throughout their bodies due to a crisis, and have weak immune systems, which causes their bodies to be unable to fight off deadly illnesses the way a normal person's can. When someone with sickle cell catches the common cold, it lingers a lot longer than it does in a person who does not have sickle cell anemia. People have said sickle cell is a lot harder for males to deal with versus females.

Many people in my lifetime have shared their personal stories about what they know about sickle cell. The most negative thing people usually share with me is that a family member of theirs died due to having sickle cell anemia. They always tell me the person died at a young age. I have a lot of people tell me I might not live long. It is hard to hear that many people feel sorry for me and others who suffer from sickle cell anemia. I don't like for people to feel sorry for me or have a pity party for me; I'm a survivor. I tell them my mother always encouraged me to try to stay positive.

For me, the hardest thing about having sickle cell anemia is the unknown. I never know when I'll have an episode or crisis. They are unpredictable. I can be having a great day and feeling good, and bam—I wake up in the middle of the night or early in the morning and am in a crisis. It could be a horrific one or a mild one I can manage on my own.

Crises are like earthquakes: the bigger the magnitude, the more damage they seem to do. The bigger crises are a lot harder on my body and cause me the most pain. However, as with earthquakes, the smaller the magnitude, the less damage it does. When I have little crises, I can manage them at home with the help of over-the-counter medicines, heating pads, and medicines I rub on my body to ease some of the pain.

I think the smaller crises are better for me because I usually don't have to go to the hospital or don't have to be admitted. I don't like hospitals at all. But that is normal for people with sickle cell disease, because we frequent hospitals all our lives. I'm aware that hospitals are supposed to be places where we can go for help, but sometimes they also can be scary. I have visited many hospitals throughout my lifetime. I have seen the good, the bad, and the ugly sides of hospitals.

I have had good experiences as well as bad experiences during my hospital stays. I have been in lots of hospitals, and each one was different. I have had some wonderful experiences, including good doctors and nurses who seemed to have big hearts and truly love working in the hospitals and dealing with patients. I have had hospital staff as well as volunteers go way beyond their personal job requirements to ensure I was well taken care of. For example, I once was so dehydrated that I had to get multiple IV sticks. A nurse came into my room and stuck me in a spot that no one else had thought of, and she was able to start an IV on me. I've also had nurses who knew I had sickle cell be patient with me and rub three alcohol pads on my arm before they stuck me, because that made me a lot more comfortable. I've had nurses whose shifts ended stay to work an extra shift because they really loved to help patients. I've had nurses bring me books, magazines, and other personal items to lift my spirits. I've had nurses sit in my room to entertain me and share life-changing stories and advice. God has blessed me with some guardian angels in the form of doctors, nurses, and volunteers.

However, there I also had bad encounters. As I mentioned, there have been some hospital stays I hated. I have had some bad interactions that made me dread ever going to a hospital, period. It got so bad that I refused to go visit people in the hospital due to my being traumatized. I used to have a phobia of hospitals because of how I was treated by certain people in the hospitals. I have been in and out of hospitals from the age of five years old until now. I have had hundreds of horrible hospital visits when I was admitted and also when I wasn't admitted. Once, when I was dehydrated and they were having a difficult time getting an IV put in, some of the nurses were impatient because they were aggravated that they were unable to get an IV started. They were irritated that out of all the nurses who tried, none of them were able to stick me. I've also had nurses get quite impatient with me because I kept calling them on the patient call button. I could tell they were aggravated and irritated that I kept needing their assistance. I wasn't trying to offend them; I just needed some assistance. I also experienced a moment when a nurse gave me too much medicine through my IV, which caused me to be so sleepy that they had a difficult time attempting to wake me up. I also have experienced times in the hospital when I felt neglected because I wasn't given a bath for a few days.

I have gotten a lot better, though. I now can go visit hospitals to see sick friends and family members and be okay. I used to instantly get stressed out when I walked into a hospital. I felt if I went to visit a hospital, I'd end up being in the hospital a few days later.

My mother always told me I should always cooperate with doctors and nurses in the hospital because their main goal is to help me feel better. She encouraged me to do my best to work with the doctors and nurses, not give them a hard time, and not resist them when they were trying to help me. When I was young, I didn't understand exactly what my mama meant by that. However, now I heed those words of encouragement that my mother instilled in me as a child.

ACKNOWLEDGMENTS

I first want to thank God, who is the head of my life and the head of my home. I thank him for keeping me in his loving arms for forty-seven years.

My mother has always been my greatest doctor, nurse, counselor, and support system since I was born. My sisters have always been with me through the good, the bad, and the ugly. Thank you, Angela; Kathy; Kimberly; Earlasha, a.k.a. Lasha; and my handsome brother Kaster, who is in my heart because he is no longer here. I love and appreciate all my siblings for being with me and helping my mother take care of me when I was in crisis as a child. Thanks to my other three siblings, whom I love as well: Cee-Cee, Dee-Dee, and Ramoan. Thanks to my wonderful husband, Kenneth; my handsome son, Jayce; my stepson, Travis; my nephews, Jeff, Jordan, and Kazmir; and my nieces, Joycelyn, Vivian, Christine, Jarhonda, Kalysia, and Kynnedi, whom I love dearly. To my great-nieces and great-nephews, I love all of you too.

Thanks to my best friends, Jeannine, April, Sheila, and Alyssa, who have been there for me as I battle to survive this horrific disease. I have way too many friends, so if you know me and have played a major role in my life, I love you too. If I omitted anyone, please charge it to my mind and not my heart.

Last but not least, thanks to my student Logan James Meadows, who let me know to strive every day to be regular regardless of what life has in store for me.

CHAPTER 1

Life-Changing Diagnosis

I was born in Waco, Texas, in 1973. During that time, the state of Texas did not test babies for sickle cell anemia. My mother was raising four daughters, and one of them was sick. She had no clue I had a life-threatening illness. My mother said that when I was a few months old, I would cry more so than usual, but she had no clue I was in a crisis. She said I would be fussy and not eat at times. My mother had had three children prior to my being born and knew how to take care of them, but I was not an ordinary child. I was a child who needed extra care due to my having sickle cell anemia. My mother said she told her parents I always complained about pains in my back and my legs. My grandfather said I was probably having growing pains.

My mother decided she wanted to move to California. When we moved to San Francisco, I was only five years old. One day my mother told my sisters and me that we were going to see a doctor for a checkup. I was freaking out because I was petrified of needles. I hated them with a passion. I rode the city bus with my mother and my sisters to a clinic near Mission Street in San Francisco. I was nervous and anxious to get the checkup over with because my mother had told me we would all be getting a blood test.

As we got closer to the hospital, my nerves were in total stress mode. I kept asking my mother, "Are we there yet?" I needed to know because I was hatching a plan to run as soon as we exited the city bus.

We got off the bus and walked into the clinic. My older three sisters got their shots and were done. Then my little sister, who was two years younger than I, got her shot. However, when it was my turn to get my shot, I decided to be difficult and attempted to run away. I decided to bolt out of the clinic. My older three sisters chased after me and dragged me back. The nurses physically held me down while I received a blood test.

I screamed and hollered as if I were being murdered by a serial killer. My mother tried to reason with me, but her attempts fell on deaf ears, and I acted a complete fool. I was put in a straitjacket whenever I needed blood drawn from that day forward, until I turned thirteen years old.

They gave me the blood test, and we went home. I told my mom I hated blood tests and never wanted another one in my life.

My mother smiled and said, "You probably will have to get some more blood tests in your life. But they will not be bad." She also said, "You did a great job." But in reality, I know I did horribly.

My mother later said we all had to go back to the clinic to get the blood test results to make sure we were all healthy. I smiled because I knew I was healthy—or so I thought.

We went to the clinic, and the doctor called us all back to his office. I sat in the doctor's office smiling because I knew I was not getting another blood test. However, I was wrong.

The doctor told my mother, "I have some good news and some bad news."

My eyes got big. Although I was only five years old, I knew what good news and bad news meant.

He said, "Two of your daughters have what is known as the sickle cell trait. And one of your daughters has the actual disease. Two of your daughters are normal and have nothing wrong with them at all."

When the doctor said I was the one with sickle cell, I almost fainted—I was shocked. I started crying. I did not know exactly what sickle cell anemia was, but I knew if it was a disease, it was not good. My mother walked over and hugged me. She reassured me I was going to be okay. But I kept crying. My four sisters said, "You will be all right because we will be with you."

What the doctor said next almost killed me instantly. He said I had sickle cell anemia, a blood disorder. He said my blood cells were shaped like sickles, not round like a normal person's cells. He said, "When a healthy person's cells are moving, they pass by each other. But sickle cells touch each other and stick to one another. It causes the person to go through what is called a sickle cell crisis."

It is as if my cells are a car at a stoplight. When I am not in a crisis, the light is green, and my cells are just driving along the road. When the light turns yellow, my cells are slowing down. But when they are at a red light, my cells are completely stopped—and that is when I am in a crisis.

He then began explaining exactly what sickle cell disease was. He stated it was a blood disorder that primarily affected African Americans. He said other cultures could get it if they had African American blood in their family blood line. He told my mother, "Sickle cell was first discovered in Africa. Africans either had malaria fever or sickle cell. Sickle cell fights malaria fever. If malaria fever came to the United States, she wouldn't contract it, because the two illnesses can't coexist in the body at the same time." He had a smirk on his face when he said, "Well, look at the bright side: she will not ever have to worry about getting malaria fever."

The next words that came out of his mouth knocked me to my knees. He said, "Most people who have sickle cell usually do not live past seventeen years old. They usually die incredibly young. Just try to give her the best life you possibly can."

I looked at him as if he were crazy. I just kept hearing that I was going to only live to be seventeen years old, and then I was going to die. I immediately started crying because that was a lot for a five-year-old child to take in. I thought I was going to live for only twelve more years, and then I was going to die.

To know you are going to die is hard, but to hear you are going to die young is even harder. The doctor had put an expiration date on my life. I was hysterical and unable to gain my composure. My mama grabbed me and said, "You will not die at seventeen! Only God knows when you will die. God has you, and he will take you when he is ready." She hugged me and reassured me that I was going to be okay. I wiped my tears because I knew my mother was right. She was always right and always made sure I was okay.

The doctor said, "I suggest you take her to a regular hospital, because they have doctors who are hematologists and who specialize in sickle cell anemia. Once she gets established with that hospital, she will get the treatment she needs to live her life with sickle cell anemia. Sickle cell anemia is hereditary and is passed down through the blood line. Two people who have the sickle cell trait can create a child with sickle cell disease. One parent with the sickle cell trait and one parent with sickle cell disease can create a child with sickle cell disease. A parent who has sickle cell disease can create a child with the sickle cell trait, because the parent with the disease can pass on the trait to his or her child. That person is known as a carrier."

He told my mother that a hematologist would educate us all a lot more when we went to see one at the hospital. He mentioned that crises were generally triggered by cold weather. He suggested I stay warm and try to avoid extreme cold weather at all times. He said, "Always make sure she drinks a lot of water and stays well hydrated. She will need to take folic acid pills. They are vitamins for people who are anemic. When a sickle cell person has a crisis, it is usually treated with oxygen, morphine, and an IV drip, which will usually hydrate the person."

Crises are painful episodes that can occur quite often, depending on the person who suffers from sickle cell anemia. Depending on the crisis, an individual might deal with it at home or might need to go to the hospital because it is unbearable. A crisis can be so bad that a person can die due to a painful sickle cell crisis. Sickle cell is a deadly, life-threatening disease that takes a lot of people's lives. It is a serious disease that, in my opinion, does not get enough recognition. It is a predominantly African American disease that has been around for centuries. However, anyone who has any percentage of black in them can be born with sickle cell anemia. There are people of different cultures who suffer from sickle cell due to having some origin of black in them and their family. It is just as deadly as cancer, leukemia, lupus, AIDS, and other treacherous diseases.

As a child, at different stores, I saw donation cans for different diseases; however, I never saw a can for my disease. It used to make me cry when I saw how unimportant my disease was to everyone other than myself and people who shared the disease with me. I feel as if I am responsible for myself as well as all the other people who have sickle cell anemia. My disease is an important part of who I am. I thank God for my disease because I could have been born with something much worse.

I complained one day because I was in a bad mood and was angry because I had to go to the hospital to get a blood test. My mother grabbed me by the hand and walked me to the cancer ward, where I saw lots of children who looked a lot sicker than I was. My mother told me, "Those children"—she pointed to the cancer patients—"are not only sick but also lose their hair and must have radiation and chemotherapy. You need to count your blessings, because it could be worse. Take a good look at those children; be thankful you are not as sick as they are." My mama made realize I was blessed and needed to count all my blessings. My mama helped me put my life in perspective.

CHAPTER 2

Sickle Cell Crises and Blood Transfusions

I have met a lot of people in my life, and the number-one question they ask is "How does a crisis feel?" I usually smile, sigh, pause for a moment, and then say, "When I'm in a sickle cell crisis, it feels like someone is stabbing me all over my body with a large kitchen knife a million times. I am in excruciating pain, which is unbearable. The pain is so bad that I wish God would just take me, because I would not be in as much pain. The pain is so difficult that being dead seems a lot easier than the pain I have to endure."

When I was younger, I used to pray that God would take me so I would not have to be in any more pain. However, I knew my mother loved me and needed me. I knew my four sisters and my little brother would have been sad and miserable without me. I loved my family so much that I fought even harder when I went into a crisis.

Once my son was born, I knew I had to fight harder than I had ever fought before, because God had allowed me to become a mother to a little baby boy who needed me more than anyone else in my life. My prayer changed, and I started praying for strength to make it through all my crises. I no longer wanted God to take me, but I wanted him to keep me healthy so I could be the best mother I could be to my son. My son has the trait, due to my being a carrier.

While growing up, I met some other children who suffered from sickle cell anemia just as I did. When I was about thirteen years old, my mother encouraged me to go to what was known back in the day as sickle cell camp. My sickle cell counselor suggested I go mingle with other sickle cell children. I did not want to go, because my little sister was not allowed to go, as she did not have sickle cell. I felt I would be a lot more comfortable if she was allowed to go with me.

At sickle cell camp, I met two sisters who were black and white, and they both had sickle cell. They were only three years apart in age. I basically stayed with them the whole week at sickle cell camp. I met them on the bus ride on our way to camp. I sat across from them on the bus. I asked them, "How does it feel when you are in a crisis?"

They looked at each other, and one said, "It feels like I'm being stabbed with a knife."

I said, "Wow, that is exactly how I feel."

The older sister said, "I think all sickle cell people feel the same exact way that we do."

Our camp counselor was a few years older than I, and she also had sickle cell. I asked her the same question I'd asked the two sisters, and she said she'd be in a lot of pain and feel as if she were being stabbed with a knife. She verified the two sisters' and my thoughts about how a crisis felt. I met quite a few children at camp who also verified how they felt when they were in a crisis.

It amazed me that we all had the same horrific disease and that it affected us all in the same manner. I have also watched many videos and read personal testimonies from people who suffer from sickle cell, and almost every one of them has verified exactly how I feel when I am in a crisis.

I have had a few relatives who suffered from sickle cell and passed on. I have other people in my family who suffer from sickle cell as well. However, sickle cell affects each individual in different ways, because there are different levels of sickle cell. Some people who have sickle cell have physical identifiers, such as eyes that have a yellow tint to them, a symptom that imitates jaundice but is part of sickle cell disease. Some people's eyes will have a slight yellow tint to them when they are about to go through a crisis. Some people get crises in their heads and suffer from painful headaches. The headaches mimic migraines and cause a lot of pain. I have leg, back, and arm pain in my joints. I also have what imitates a heart attack, which is known as a chest crisis. I usually go to the hospital when I am experiencing a chest pain, because it usually means I am dehydrated.

People who have sickle cell may have different types of symptoms. Some symptoms will be similar, and some symptoms may differ.

Most sickle cell patients have had several blood transfusions. I thank God for people who have saved the lives of myself and others who suffer from sickle cell by being blood donors. I know that without someone giving me blood, I would not be able to share my personal journey with anyone.

When I was younger, I was not as mature or as educated on blood transfusions as I am currently. I used to be ignorant and thought I was going to contract AIDS or some other horrible disease due to getting some stranger's blood. However, as I got older and researched blood transfusions, I became a lot more educated as well as comfortable.

When I got my first blood transfusion, I was about nineteen years old. I was sick and had been in the hospital for a few weeks. The doctor who was taking care of me came into my room and said, "We are going to have to give you a blood transfusion."

I looked at him as if he were crazy. When he asked me if I'd ever had a blood transfusion, I answered with a mean demeanor, "No. I do not want anyone else's blood running through my body, especially a stranger's. Whose blood will I be getting? What color are they? Are they young or old?"

He smiled and said, "Blood donors are anonymous."

I asked, "Why won't you just tell me whose blood will be running through my veins?"

He sat down in a chair and explained to me what a blood donor did and how a transfusion worked.

Even after the doctor explained the process to me, I still felt uneasy about the fact that I was going to have a stranger's blood running through my veins. I began to cry. I picked up the phone and called my mama. My mama asked me what was wrong. I was crying and upset. My mother encouraged me to calm down. I told my mama I refused to get a blood transfusion.

My mama said, "You will get that blood transfusion. Do you hear me?" I knew my mama was getting upset with me at that moment. She said, "I'm heading up to the hospital."

My mama was at work, and her shift had not ended. She hung up, and I knew she was mad.

After my mama hung up, my hospital phone rang. I picked up the phone, and it was my little brother. He said, "I love you. Mama called and told me you do not want to get a blood transfusion."

I explained to him that I was uncomfortable and did not want to get a stranger's blood.

He said, "We love you; we need you to be here. Just take the blood transfusion." He sounded sad.

I told him, "Okay, I will do it." He convinced me to get the blood transfusion.

After I hung up with my little brother, my mama walked into my hospital room. She hugged me. I told her my little brother had called me and convinced me to accept the blood transfusion. She smiled and reassured me that I was going to be fine.

I do not remember how many blood transfusions I have had, but I have had quite a few, and I thank God for all my donors. I even watch the blood go in when they give me a blood transfusion. I am amazed that someone can save my life just by donating some of his or her blood to me.

CHAPTER 3

Physical and Emotional Battle

I have had many crises in my forty-seven years of life. It would be too long and tedious to attempt to discuss each and every last one with people. I have had hundreds of crises in my life; some were severe, some were mild, and some were manageable. The severity depends on the different types of crises I go through.

For example, with the ones I think are severe, I always go to the emergency room and usually am hospitalized. When I am admitted, I routinely get Demerol, morphine, or Dilantin. They always have to give me an IV so they can rehydrate me. They also give me an oxygen mask so I can breathe more easily. If my blood is low, I will get a blood transfusion too.

If a crisis feels mild, I may go to the emergency room, but I usually am sent home and not hospitalized. Mild crises are usually manageable at home. In such a crisis, my joints hurt, and my lower or upper back, legs, or arms hurt. I take pain medicines, such as Tylenol, ibuprofen, or any type of medicine that can mask the pain for a few hours. The pain medicine does not completely take away the pain; it just makes the pain seem controllable for a little while.

The first crisis I can recall happened when I was eight years old. We lived in Waco, Texas. We had moved back to Texas because my mother's mom had to get her leg amputated due to diabetes complications. At the time, my mother had five daughters only; my little brother had not been born yet. She was a single mother raising five daughters all alone. I thank her for doing anything she could to make a better life for me and my siblings. She made many sacrifices to ensure we would be able to make it as adults.

I was in third grade, and my class was going to go on a field trip to see the movie *ET*. I was excited to see the movie, but my excitement was short-lived. I ended up having a severe crisis. I was so sick that I was unable to walk for about two weeks.

My grandmother nursed me back to health. She would rub my joints I had pains in. She would rub me down with Bengay and alcohol, and she would have me lie on a heating pad. She did not take me to the hospital.

I was always sick, but I had my favorite two ladies by my bedside. It was bittersweet because I was happy I was being cared for by them, but I hated the pain I was in. I enjoyed all the attention I was getting, but being sick was a bummer. I hated missing school and not seeing my friends. I had the best of both worlds. It was unique to see how my grandmother was so capable of taking care of me, and she had a prosthetic leg. She was an amazing woman. She ended up dying five years later, when I was only thirteen years old. She has been gone for thirty-four years, and I still miss her like crazy. My heart yearns for her.

My mother was not given a book on how to take care of a sick child, let alone a child with sickle cell anemia. Everything she did for me she had to learn on her own. No one taught me how to deal with sickle cell anemia but my mother. She made sure I was educated on my disease. She wanted me to research all I could so I would know about it. She wanted me to know as much as most doctors knew so I would be able to assist doctors as they took care of me. I read a lot of books about sickle cell anemia—all the books available when I was a child. There was not much research available when I was a little girl. As a forty-seven-year-old woman now, I find there still is not enough information out in the world about sickle cell anemia.

Sickle cell anemia is not only a physical disease but an emotional disease as well. I say that it is an emotional disease because I have to be able to be strong in some rough times. The disease can have me in an emotional state. There are times when I do not know whether I'm coming or going. I try to pretend I am no different from any other woman, but unlike many other women, I was born with a life-threatening disease.

If I did not tell people I have sickle cell anemia, no one would know. I do not look like I have sickle cell anemia. I look normal. There is no unusual look I have that alerts other people who do not know me that I have sickle cell anemia.

I used to hide the fact that I had sickle cell anemia, because I did not feel like explaining what sickle cell anemia was. I would wait until I had been sick and in a crisis and had recovered, and that was when I would tell people I had sickle cell anemia.

When I was a teenager, I was not allowed to date until I was sixteen years old. However, when I was in high school, my friends and I would go around calling guys we liked our boyfriend. I was talking to one guy one day, and we both liked each other. I did not tell him I had sickle cell, because I felt he did not need to know. Well, you know how messy people can be in high school. Some of the people in my school were aware that I had sickle cell. However, some people had no clue I had a disease at all. He said, "You did not tell me?"

I said, "You are not my real boyfriend, and besides, I can tell whoever I want to tell or not tell whoever I do not want to tell." I walked away.

He said, "We are done."

I laughed and said, "Good, because we were never together for real anyway."

He stopped speaking with me. I did not know he was going to be so angry that I had not told him. When I was younger, I'd tell only people I felt comfortable telling.

However, now that I'm older and a lot more mature, I'm comfortable telling anyone who knows me that I have sickle cell. It is a major part of who I am. I think if I did not have sickle cell, my life might not have the purpose that it has because I have the disease. It makes my life a lot more worth living. I embrace all facets of life. I do not have sickle cell anemia; sickle cell anemia has me.

CHAPTER 4

Hospitalizations

My little brother was born in Houston, Texas. Afterwards, we moved back to San Francisco, California. My mother felt California was a better place for us to live because it had a lot more benefits to offer our family than Texas did.

When I was ten years old, I had a severe crisis that caused me to be hospitalized. I was in the hospital for about a week. My mother was not able to stay overnight at the hospital with me, but she was there by my bedside every day. She would come see me early in the morning. We had a car, but my mom always said, "It's better to go in an ambulance because it will help you to get into the back room quicker." She was right. When I drive myself to the hospital, I usually must wait in the waiting room much longer than if I had called 911 and been driven to the hospital by an ambulance. However, now that I'm older, I usually have my husband just drive me, and I just wait until I am called to the back.

My mother taught me a lot about how to deal with hospitals as well as with doctors regarding my sickle cell anemia. She wanted me to be just as educated as my doctors when I was in a crisis, so I could explain to them what they should do for me. She said, "Please learn as much as you can about sickle cell anemia so you can educate others."

I had been in the hospital for a week and was released. My mom and I headed to the place where we were staying with my three sisters, my little brother, and my stepdad. We rode in a taxi from the hospital. The hospital had given my mama vouchers to go back and forth to the hospital when she had to take me.

It was hard to stay the night at the hospital, especially all by myself. I hated being alone. I wanted to be home with my siblings. The hospital was lonely. I had a hard time sleeping at night. I would toss and turn a lot. My siblings would come visit me sometimes, and I would be ecstatic to see them. I looked forward to seeing them when they came to the hospital.

The hospital was a creepy place at night. I saw lots of people walking back and forth through the hospital. I did not like that the hospital was so open. I felt as if anyone could just walk into a hospital right off the street, and no one would ever know. I felt the hospital lacked a lot of security. I thought a serial killer could just walk into my hospital room and get me.

Leaving the hospital, I was happy to be going home to be with my siblings. We lived in a low-income hotel; three of my sisters and I lived in one room across the hallway from my mom, my little brother, and my stepdad. It was cool because it was as if we had our own apartment. But my mother and my little brother were always in our room.

We ended up moving to a low-income housing project in San Francisco. It was one of the roughest projects in the city. My mother decided we needed to move so we could start a new life. We were not used to living in the projects, because in Waco, Texas, we always had lived in a house. We lived in low-income projects for about two years prior to having to move back to Waco, Texas, due to my grandmother having to get her leg amputated.

The projects were a different type of environment than my family was used to. My mother was raising six children all by herself, with no assistance from any of our fathers. She was extraordinarily strong, because she took care of all of us by herself, including having a sick child like me to care for as well.

When we moved to the projects and were the new family on the block, we did not know anyone, and that was awkward. However, in a few days, we made a lot of new friends. My best friend and I met in the projects and are still friends and have been for the past thirty-seven years. We are more like sisters. When I told her I had sickle cell anemia, she had no clue what it was. None of my friends in the projects were aware of what sickle cell anemia was. I educated all of them about my disease. Afterward, they always made sure I dressed and stayed warm. When I was sick and in the hospital, I always had a roomful of friends and family visit me. The hospital staff did not like that I had a roomful of teenagers, but they were my friends, and I needed them there. I felt better when I was surrounded by my siblings and friends. Their presence made the hospital stay a lot easier.

I once had an out-of-body experience while I was having surgery. I don't like to share my out-of-body experience with people, because many either don't believe me or just think I was hallucinating. I don't like to go under anesthesia, because I do not do well when I am being forced to go to sleep. I do not like the unnatural sleep state. I like to go to sleep on my own.

When I was about ten years old, I was getting some tubes put in my ears due to my not being able to hear. During the surgery, I had an out-of-body experience and physically floated out of my body. I could see myself lying on the operating table and the doctors conducting surgery on me. I remember realizing I had the ability to float up into the air.

I floated up into the air and drifted past different rooms, searching for my mama and my little sister. I saw other patients in their rooms as I glided by. After searching different rooms, I finally found my mama. I tried to get my mother's and little sister's attention. I tried to do so by yelling. I said, "Mama, look up here! I'm here!" I screamed my little sister's name, but she was unable to hear me as well. I was frustrated that they were unable to hear me or see me. But I was able to hear their conversation.

My little sister asked my mama why I was almost always sick. My mama explained to her that I had sickle cell anemia and was always sick because of painful episodes known as crises. My little sister was only eight years old and couldn't quite figure out why I was always in and out of hospitals. My mama was looking at a magazine while waiting for my surgery to be over. However, my little sister kept asking my mama a lot of questions, so she had to put the magazine down and try to further explain my condition to her.

After my surgery was over, I couldn't wait to see my mama and little sister. When I was rolled back into my hospital room, my mama and little sister were sitting in my room, waiting for me. I was excited to see them both. I told my mama that I had something to tell her. I was excited to share my out-of-body experience with her and my little sister. When I told my mother about my out-of-body experience, she gave me a peculiar look; however, when I told her verbatim exactly what she had said, she knew I was telling the truth, because I had been in surgery and had not been with her and my little sister when they had their conversation.

CHAPTER 5

Thirteenth Birthday

My thirteenth birthday was scary for me because I knew that in four short years, I would possibly be gone due to sickle cell anemia. I had a lot of mixed emotions running through my body. I was happy because it was my birthday but sad because I was turning one year older. I just wanted to stay twelve years old forever and never age again.

My mama bought me a fancy calculator that I begged her to buy me from a major department store. She also bought me some other things. When I woke up that morning, I was not excited, as I usually was on my birthday. My mama asked me, "What is wrong? You should be ecstatic because it is your birthday and a special birthday at that."

I managed a weak smile and said, "Mama, all my birthdays are special because God keeps blessing me to live another year. But my time will be running out in a few years."

My mama said, "No one knows when their time will run out. Only God knows, and he holds your life in his hands. He will take you when he sees fit. Stop worrying, and start living. You only live once. You must start living life for today and not focus on tomorrow." She hugged me and added, "I know that you will live to be over seventeen years old and for an exceptionally long time."

After my mama said that, I instantly felt much better. My mama always knew just what to say and exactly what I needed to hear.

I went outside, and all my friends told me happy birthday. I was happy that so many people were giving me birthday wishes. I realized that not only did my family love me, but a lot of my friends loved me so much too.

My best friend, Jeannine, hugged me and reassured me that I would be fine and told me to stop worrying so much.

I had a doctor's appointment the day after my birthday, which I was not ready for, because as I've mentioned, I hate needles and am a difficult stick due to having sickle cell anemia. People with sickle cell anemia get so many shots that they tend not to be a big fan of needles. I was basically traumatized as a child, and I really fear needles. As I've mentioned, I had to be put in a straitjacket because I was a difficult stick. The nurses used to hate to see me and my mama coming to the clinic. They used to have the straitjacket ready for me when I arrived at the clinic.

I decided to get dressed up all nice, so I put on a dress. My mama looked at me strangely. She said, "Why are you dressed like that? You know they are going to put you in a straitjacket."

I smiled at her.

She said, "What are you up to?"

I said, "Nothing, Mama," with a sneaky smile.

My mama knew me better than anyone else in my life. She knew I was up to something.

We rode the bus to the hospital, and I was quiet. I am a lot of things, but quiet is not something I am. I love to talk; I talk to anyone who will listen to me. I was born to talk. I have always been an extrovert. My mama kept looking at me during the whole bus ride. When we got to the hospital, I walked in as if I were a model. The nurses came out with the straitjacket. I told them they did not need it, because I was now a young lady. "I am more mature and realize that you guys are only here to help me."

My mama looked at me like "Who are you, and where is my daughter? Who the heck are you?"

I smiled at my mama. I said, "I'm good. You always tell me that the nurses and doctors are here to support and help me. I woke up and decided I should help them and not fight against them." I walked over, sat down, and stuck my arm out so they could draw my blood.

My mama stood there with a weird look on her face. The two nurses who had the straitjacket stood there in case I was pretending I was going to cooperate. A nurse came out, put the tourniquet on me, and drew my blood. It hurt, but I did not even flinch, because I had to prove to them that I was a woman of my word. My mama said, "Good job, Klee." I looked over at her and smiled.

We walked out of the clinic, and as we were walking out, all the nurses were looking and whispering and pointing at me. I'd shown them I was now a teenager and did not need a straitjacket anymore.

When we got home, my mother was proud of me. She walked into our house bragging to all my siblings about how well I had done at the clinic. She told them I did not have to be put in a straitjacket because I was now a more mature young lady. All my siblings were astonished and amazed that I did not have to be restrained. My siblings knew that when it came to my going to any clinic and getting a shot, I was going to act a complete fool.

My little sister said, "You are talking about her, Mama?" She pointed to me.

My mama said, "Yes, she did a great job, and I'm so proud of her."

One of my older sisters looked at me, smiled, and said, "Wow, good job." She used to have to take me to the clinic sometimes to get my monthly checkup, and I would act a fool. She would have to chase me because I would run.

Once, when I was about eight years old, when we lived in Houston, Texas, my mother was taking us all to the clinic. I knew I was going to have to get a blood test, so as we got closer to the hospital, I decided to run. I ran over an overpass and could have gotten seriously hurt or even hit by a car in trying to avoid getting a blood test. My older sister chased me and dragged me back kicking and screaming to the clinic.

CHAPTER 6

Six-Month Hospital Stay

When I was fourteen years old, I had a rough crisis. It was two o'clock in the morning, and I started having chest pains. I was in a chest crisis. I did not want to wake my mama up, so I took it upon myself to get my own medicine. I accidentally took two tablespoons instead of two teaspoons.

I went and lay back down in my bed. I almost overdosed because I took too much medicine. Even though I wasn't a little child, I should have gone to get my mother before I took that medicine. No one under eighteen years of age needs to ever administer medicine.

After lying down for about ten minutes, I felt my pain start to get worse. I had to go wake my mama up. She asked me what was wrong. I told her, "I took Tylenol, but I am still in a lot of pain."

My mama jumped up and got dressed. She called 911, and I got dressed while we were waiting for the ambulance to arrive. I was on the couch, lying down, crying uncontrollably because I was in excruciating pain. The pain was so bad I was hollering. I woke up my entire house. My three sisters and my little brother all walked into the living room to see what the commotion was. My mama told them, "Go back to sleep. Your sister is in a crisis, and we are on our way to the hospital." My siblings all hugged me and reassured me that I would be fine. They all went back to bed.

The ambulance arrived, and they put me on a gurney, took me down three flights of stairs, and put me in the ambulance. My mama climbed into the ambulance, and we were en route to the hospital. My mama held my hand all the way there. Although I was in pain, Mama's being there made my pain seem a little more bearable. The hospital was only fifteen minutes away, but it seemed as if we were in the ambulance for about two hours.

Upon our arrival at the hospital, I was happy because I knew the doctors would get me out of pain. Boy, was I wrong, because when the EMTs took me into the hospital, they rolled the gurney into the emergency room. I thought they were going to just roll me into the back and put me in a room. My mama went to the front desk and told them I was in a lot of pain and needed to see a doctor immediately.

The lady behind the desk said, "Ma'am, I understand that your little girl is in a lot of pain, but we have to wait for a doctor."

My mama was getting frustrated with the lady because I was now on the floor, rolling around like a fish flopping out of water. I was screaming at the top of my lungs. Everyone in the emergency room waiting area stared at me as if I were crazy.

An older white doctor walked out, and he walked up to my mother. He held out his hand and introduced himself to my mama. The look on my mama's face told me she was upset. My mother did not want to shake his hand, but because of how her mama had raised her, she knew it was the right thing to do. What he said next blew me and my mama away. He said, "I'm going to take her to the back and give her some pain medicine, but I would like to observe her for about thirty minutes."

My mama looked at him like "Are you crazy? Look at my baby." I remember him looking at me as if I were an animal or alien. He observed me, and then he had some nurses come assist me back onto my gurney. They rolled me back to a room. My mama was as hot as fish grease. She was fuming. No mama wants to see her child in pain, especially when she cannot even help her child.

As if I were not in enough pain already, I was completely dehydrated. I felt as if I were having a heart attack. I was in a chest crisis. I had not been drinking enough water. The doctor came into the room, and I looked at him as if he were crazy, because it was the older white guy who had just sat there watching me in distress. My mama's whole mood shifted when he walked into my room. He asked how I was doing. My mama gave him a deadly look. He knew my mama was upset. He said, "I will get an IV line started and give her some morphine and oxygen so we can get her back home as soon as possible."

However, he did not get me home for six months. Yes, I was in the hospital for six long months. That is the longest time I have ever been in the hospital. I was in there for half a year.

I thought I would be out of pain quickly, but boy, was I wrong. A nurse came in to put an IV in, but she could not get it. She tried two more times, and then she gave up. She sent in five or six more nurses, and they also were unable to give me an IV. I got stuck twenty-seven times and was ready to just give up, until an angel walked into my room. She walked in and introduced herself. I do not remember what she looked like, but I know she was Spanish. She walked in and said, "I will stick you once, and if I do not get it, I will stop." She had an infectious smile. She had a beautiful glow, and I immediately felt at peace and a sense of calmness came over me. I knew she was sent from heaven by God himself. She was a gentle spirit. She was kind and careful with me. She put the tourniquet on my arm, and she said, "You will feel a little sting and a poke, and I will be done." She was able to get it.

She smiled, and I smiled, even though I was pain. I said, "Thank you; you did it."

She said, "No, thank you; you did it. You were so brave. I do not think I could have gotten stuck as many times as you did. Good job, young lady." She gave me a hug, and she walked out of the room.

I hugged my mama. Another nurse walked into the room and hooked my IV into the machine and added fluids and morphine so I would get better.

The next six months were exceedingly long and boring. I was a fourteen-year-old little girl stuck in a hospital bed and not allowed to go home. I hated hospitals, and now I was forced to be a six-month regular tenant and patient in one. I hated hospitals because the nurses were always poking and prodding me all the time. I felt more like a guinea pig than a patient because every day I got blood tests, and they ran all kinds of tests on me. I was already skinny when I arrived at the hospital, but after six months, I had lost a lot more weight. I could not afford to lose any more. I refused to eat their horrible food. My little sister and one of my friends would come to the hospital and eat my food, and I would pretend I had eaten it. But

I was not fooling anyone but myself, because I was losing weight instead of gaining it. The doctor knew because I was getting thinner and thinner.

I was not able to walk after lying in that bed for so long. I became bedridden. I had to go to physical therapy every day so I could learn how to walk again and regain my strength. I had my own personal physical therapist who came and got me every day and worked with me for six months until I was back on my feet.

Prior to my getting sick and going to the hospital, my little sister and I had been planning to go see a world-famous singer in concert. However, we were going to have to cancel going to the event, because I was still sick. I loved the singer and would have done anything to see him, because I loved him so much. I knew the concert was in three weeks, and I had to get better so I could go home. I knew if I was at home, my mother would allow me to go.

I decided to eat the food at the hospital so I could gain a few pounds, and they would assume I was getting better. I asked my doctor, "What do I need to do to go home?"

He said, "You have to get better." Then he would let me go home.

I was quite the charmer; I convinced him I was 100 percent better.

He said, "Okay, I will make you a deal. If you eat all your food and get stronger, you may go home."

They allowed me to go home two days before the concert. Well, I was happy and excited to get out of that hospital, but I ended up going right back the day after the concert.

I went to the concert, and while we were there, a fight broke out, and a large riot happened. My little sister and I had to run for our lives. To make a long story short, I had an immediate setback. It caused me to get readmitted to the hospital for two more months. I should not have left the hospital in the first place, but I wanted to go to that concert so much.

My best friend and her little brother would walk thirty minutes to the hospital to visit me every day and then another thirty minutes back to their house. She would bring him to the hospital to see me, and her brother was about five years old, so that was an exceedingly long walk for a little boy. He would come plop his little body right onto my bed and relax until it was time for them to walk back home. I would save the snacks served with my lunch for him. He would eat them while my friend and I talked. They would visit with me for two hours.

It has been thirty-seven years, and she is still my best friend and always by my side. Now, when I go into the hospital, she is not able to be present due to her having children; however, she is always available by phone. When I call her, she answers and gives me words of encouragement. I am glad she has always been there for me.

One night during my six-month hospital stay, I had an encounter with what I will call an angel. It was eleven thirty, and visiting hours were over. I was asleep, and then I woke up and decided to watch a little TV until I got sleepy. I watched the nurses walk back and forth by my door in between watching a show on the TV. Suddenly, I looked to the right side of my bed, which was near the window, and I saw an older black man leaning near my bed, on the bed rail. I looked at him and figured I was dreaming. I wiped my eyes, and no, I was not dreaming: there was a man in my room.

I sat straight up in my bed. I said, "Who are you, and why are you in my room?"

He looked at me and smiled. He said, "I'm Grandpa. I am here to let you know that you will be fine."

I looked away for a few seconds, and just like that, he was gone. I got a little frightened. I immediately grabbed my call button to reach my nurse. She asked me, "What do you need?"

I asked her to please just come. She was there in a few seconds. She walked into the room and asked me what was wrong. I looked at her and said, "There was an older black man in my room a few minutes ago. He scared me."

She looked around and said, "Where was he?"

"Standing right there," I said, pointing to the right side of my bed.

She said, "Are you sure?"

I bobbed my head up and down like a bobblehead doll.

She looked around and even checked my bathroom. She said, "Please tell me what he looked like."

I said, "Well, he was black like me, and he was an older man."

She looked around as if I were crazy, and I could see in her eyes that she did not believe a word coming out of my mouth. She went into my bathroom to see if he was in there. She came out of my bathroom and said, "Are you sure someone was here in your room?"

I was getting aggravated. I yelled, "I told you that an older black man was just standing right there!" I pointed to the right side of my bed, near the bed rail.

She looked as if she had seen a ghost. She looked a lot more scared than I was.

I said, "I am not crazy; I know what I saw. He had a real short haircut, and he had on a green striped shirt, blue jeans, and a light brown jacket."

She said, "What did he do to you?"

I said, "He did not do anything to me."

"What did he say to you?"

"He just stood there, and he smiled at me. When I asked him who he was, he said, 'I'm Grandpa, and I just came to tell you that you will be fine.'"

She looked at me with a horrific look, and she said, "Okay. If he comes back, please call me, and I will come back. By the way, no one is allowed in the hospital after eight o'clock. The security guard downstairs does not allow anyone up here after hours." Then she quickly walked out of the room as if she were escaping from a killer.

I kept looking over at the right side of my bed, where he had been leaning on my bed rail. I was scared. I slept with the TV and the lights on that night. I know there was a man in my room that night. It was odd, though, because the hospital had strict visiting hour policies. I could not wait until the morning time came, because I had to tell my mama what had happened. I knew she was going to believe me. What did I see—a ghost or a guardian angel? Who or whatever he was scared me.

My grandmother always told me God would send me a guardian angel if I ever was scared. I believe he was a guardian angel, because he had a beautiful smile on his face the whole time. He seemed to be a nice man, but he just appeared out of nowhere, and that was why I was frightened.

CHAPTER 7

Seventeen

The day I had been dreading all my life finally arrived. On March 21, 1990, I turned seventeen years old. I woke up and ran to find out where my mama was. My mother was in the kitchen, cooking breakfast for me and my siblings. I walked into the kitchen, and my mama smiled at me. She said, "Happy birthday." I smiled. She said, "I told you God was going to keep you here. You will do and can do anything you want to do in this world; you are no different from any other young lady. You will get an education, you will get married, you will have children, and you will live a normal life like any other woman."

I took my mama's words to heart, and I believed I could be just like any other normal woman but with sickle cell anemia.

That was the day I decided to start really learning to live and stop worrying about dying. I stopped focusing on dying and started living for myself. From that day on, I knew I could do anything anyone else could do, even though I had sickle cell anemia.

I was in the eleventh grade and was always a horrible student. I had mostly Ds and Fs in school. I was not able to concentrate at all in school. I had ADHD, but it was undiagnosed and untreated. I decided to pray to ask God to help me get out of school. I was tired of seeing my mother's disappointed face; there were six of us, and three of us were not doing well in school. I knew I had to try a lot harder.

I tried my best, and I did it. I became a straight-A student. I was happy because I knew my mama was going to be proud. My report came in the mail, and it had all As on it. My mama was proud of me, and I was proud of me too. I graduated from high school with honors.

Prior to graduating, I had dropped out of high school and decided to go to continuation, which was also known as adult school. I was struggling in regular school, so I decided that continuation might be a better route for me. I went to school in the morning and also at night. I already had most of the credits I needed to graduate. I only needed twenty more credits in order to graduate from regular high school. I was not great in math; I had always struggled in that subject. I never had liked math, period. It's strange because I enjoy counting when I see multiple items; however, I hated math. My teacher said I shouldn't purchase my cap and gown, because I might struggle with the math section and might not pass. I bought my cap and gown anyway, and I also prayed and asked God to help me pass.

I not only passed, but I got a high score on the GED tests. I got both a GED and a diploma. I knew I could do anything I put my mind to.

My mother decided to move us from San Francisco to Sacramento. My siblings and I were mad at first, but later in life, we all realized it was one of the best decisions she could have made for her children. We were all sad when we had to move to Sacramento and leave all our friends we had made in San Francisco. We'd lived in the projects in San Francisco for seven years and were well known. I cried a lot when we first moved to Sacramento, but I adjusted to the move in a few months. When we first moved to Sacramento, we used to go back to visit San Francisco a lot, but the visits quickly became less frequent.

Sacramento was a lot better for me because it was a hotter climate. San Francisco was by the ocean and tended to be a lot colder. I had a lot more crises when we lived in San Francisco, due to the cold weather. I seemed to have a lot fewer crises in Sacramento because the weather was a lot hotter than in the Bay Area.

The first job I got in Sacramento was at a fast food restaurant. I worked in the back, flipping burgers. My little sister and I worked together and worked the same shift. I opened my first bank account.

When we had been working there for about three months, my little sister called up the restaurant to see when we would be working next. The manager explained to my sister that she was short-staffed. My sister asked me if I wanted to go help the manager out, because she sounded desperate and needed a little help. We did not live near the restaurant, and we had a twenty-five-minute walk there and back. My sister and I walked up to the restaurant, and when we got there, the manager said, "Oh, can one of you clean tables? And I need one of you to go outside and clean the parking lot," meaning pick up trash and sweep the entire parking lot. My little sister chose to clean tables, and I went outside to clean the parking lot.

I had been outside for about twenty minutes, when I saw my little sister push open the restaurant door, looking upset. The manager came out right behind her. My sister said, "Let's go."

I said, "What is wrong?"

She said, "I said let's go."

The manager said, "Are you quitting?"

My little sister said, "Yes, I quit, and so does my sister. She has sickle cell anemia and cannot be working outside in this extreme heat!" My sister threw her apron at the manager, and we walked home.

While we were walking home, I said, "Why did you quit and make me quit?"

She said, "We are not slaves; we do not have to work for her." She quit for both of us that day. The manager had been trying to force us to do the job that her maintenance people were supposed to do. My little sister found a job a few weeks later at another fast food restaurant, but I did not work for a few months.

My next job was at a gas station. My sister's boyfriend was the manager, and he got me the job. I was happy to be working once again. I was a cashier. I worked the 2:00 to 11:00 p.m. shift and the 7:00 to 3:00 a.m. shift.

I had been working there for a few weeks, when a group of Mexican guys robbed the store three nights in a row. I was scared. I told them to take whatever they wanted but please do not hurt me.

The store manager called me into the back, where he was looking at the surveillance cameras. He said, "Did you know those guys?"

I looked at him as if he were crazy. I said, "No, I do not know those guys."

He said, "You were communicating with them."

I said, "No, I was telling them to take what they want and to please not hurt me. I was scared for my life."

He was upset. I did not care how upset he was; I feared for my life. He was so mad that he decided to have me be a stocker instead of a cashier. He knew I had sickle cell anemia and was not supposed to ever get cold, but he made me go put cold sodas, water, and beers in the freezer. I went into the freezer and was in there for about thirty minutes, and I got sick that same night. I went into a crisis. I was in a crisis for about a week and unable to work.

When I came back to work, he told me to go back into the freezer and put more drinks in the freezer. I looked at him and said, "No, you go do it. I quit." He did not care about me or my disease.

I decided to go to what was known as a nanny college, and my best friend and I went to school together. We ended up going to the nanny college for two years only to realize the college was a complete scam, and our credits were fake.

I decided to go to a community college to get an AA degree in early childhood education. It took me about four years to get my AA, because I took some classes I did not need, which made me get off track. I got my BA degree in psychology three years later, and I got my master's degree three years after that. I waited two years and then took two classes toward my doctorate in leadership. However, I decided not to finish because I did not like the program. Three years after that, I got my post-master's certificate in teaching, which I just recently obtained. I recently enrolled in school again, and this fall, I'll go back to school to get a second master's degree so I can become a school psychologist. I will be in school for about three years.

I am amazed at all I have accomplished, all while having sickle cell anemia. My mama always told me, "Go out there, and get what you want." I thank my mama for pushing me, always encouraging me, and telling me I can be and do anything I want to be or do in life.

I have done quite a lot in my life, but giving birth to my son was my best accomplishment and a gift I will cherish forever.

CHAPTER 8

911

When I was eighteen years old, I had a major crisis that I thought was going to take me out. I thought I never would see my mama, my siblings, or anyone ever again. I started praying to God to please just let me live. My good friend was spending the night at my house, when I awoke with terrible chest pains. It was a chest crisis. I was in a lot of pain. I walked into the living room, where my friend was sleeping on my couch. I yelled, "I am sick! I am in a crisis!"

She hopped up quickly and said, "What should I do?"

I told her to go downstairs to get my mama. I lived in the same apartment complex as my mother, and I also lived right upstairs above her. My friend put on her shoes and ran downstairs to my mother's apartment. She was gone for like five minutes, but it felt like an hour.

I heard my mama run up the stairs, because my friend had left my front door open. My mama walked in, and I was lying on the floor, holding my chest and gasping for air because my chest hurt badly. My mama ran over and tried to help me up, but I asked her to leave me and just call 911. My mama ran over to the phone and picked it up. She looked at my friend and said, "What is the number to 911?"

My friend looked at her with a peculiar look on her face and said, "I don't know the number."

My mama and my friend were running back and forth, trying to think of the number to call 911. My mama said, "I'll call 411 to get the number from them."

I started laughing because I could not believe my mama and my friend were so disoriented that they'd forgotten the number for 911. I told my mama to bring me the phone. I dialed 911, and as the operator answered, I was laughing at my mama and my friend. I said, "How was you gonna call 411 to get the number to 911?"

The operator said, "Excuse me? Is this a joke?"

I said, "No, ma'am. I am sorry; my mama and my friend just panicked for a few minutes and forgot the number to 911."

She said, "Okay, what is the emergency?"

I could tell by her tone she was getting aggravated with me. I said, "Ma'am, this is no joke. I am in a crisis. I have sickle cell anemia, and I need an ambulance." I gave her my address.

She said, "Are you okay?"

I said, "No, I'm having trouble breathing."

She said, "Okay, I will send an ambulance right away."

I handed my mama the phone, and she hung up. My mama and my friend helped me up so I could get on the couch while I waited for the ambulance to arrive. My friend was so nervous she could not even look at me. She was traumatized because she had never witnessed me in a crisis. She went with me and my mama to the hospital that night. However, from that night on, she refused to ever spend the night at my place again. We never talked about that night again.

I was in the hospital for about three weeks, and my friend did not come back to see me. I think my crisis was just too much for her. She would call to check on me while I was in the hospital but would not come visit. I was hurt at first because I felt I needed her because we were friends, but I understood how traumatic that experience was for her.

A guy friend who was just that—a friend—came every day to see me. He would stay for hours and keep me company and make me laugh so I would not be bored. Another guy friend came to visit me every day too. They would come in shifts; one would come for like six hours, and then the other one would come for like six hours. When visiting hours were over, they would go home. My mother and my siblings would visit, and one of the guys would always be there. My mama said, "Do those boys ever go home?"

I smiled and said, "No. I'm glad they are here, Mama, because I'm never lonely."

During that visit, I had to get my first blood transfusion. An older Vietnamese nurse was my nurse on duty. I kept begging for pain medicine, and she was getting annoyed with me because she kept having to come into my room. She said, "I'm going to give you more medicine than I'm supposed to so you will sleep and stop bugging me." I think she was mumbling under her breath, but I heard her. She might not have realized I heard her. She did exactly what she'd said she was going to do.

When I woke up, there were about ten doctors and nurses in my room. A tall white doctor said, "Welcome back."

I looked at him as if he were crazy. *What does he mean "Welcome back"? I was not gone. I did not go anywhere.*

He smiled. He said, "We could not wake you up for a while, young lady. Looks like we gave you a little too much morphine."

I said, "Oh really."

I was so sick I had to have a blood transfusion. It was the first time I had ever had one. After I had my blood transfusion, I felt a little weird. I know it was a mental thing. I was struggling with the fact that I had some strange person's blood running through my veins. I watched the blood transfusion as it went into my body. I cried because I didn't want to get the blood transfusion. But I know I needed to get the blood transfusion for me to live.

The blood transfusion put my life in perspective. I learned that life is precious and short. I feel like I took life for granted, thinking I would be able to live with sickle cell anemia and never have to get assistance from someone I did not know. When I was younger, my hematologist mentioned to me that most sickle cell patients had a lot of blood transfusions in their lifetime.

CHAPTER 9

A New Job and New Challenges

When I was twenty-four years old, my life changed a lot. I quit a job at a private day-care center, and I went to work at the school district for a better opportunity. I was hired as a teacher's assistant.

I had only been working there for three months, when I had a crisis. I was in the hospital for a few weeks. I had to get another blood transfusion.

I was scared because I had not disclosed that I had sickle cell anemia, because I'd thought I would be discriminated against and not get the job. When I was in the hospital, I had to have my mother call my supervisor to let her know I was in the hospital in a crisis. I just knew my mother was going to tell me she'd fired me. However, I was wrong. My mother said my supervisor was nice and understanding. I smiled when my mother said how nice my supervisor was.

A few days later, I received a card and some flowers from my job. I thought that was nice of them since I was a brand-new employee. I had just started and did not know a lot of people yet. It was a bad crisis, because I was unable to work for two months after my crisis. I was new, so I did not have a lot of sick days, because I had not accumulated any yet.

My supervisor called me at the hospital to check on me. I was nervous because I thought she was going to mention my not telling her I had sickle cell. I was waiting for her to tell me not to come back. However, she said, "I am aware that you do not have a lot of sick-leave days because you are new. I will solicit sick days from the other employees who work with you. Please do not worry; we take care of our people because we are one big, happy family. Just please get better. We are all praying for a speedy recovery for you, young lady."

I thanked her for the flowers and the card. I told her to please thank all the other staff as well. I had my mother go to the store to get a thank-you card. My mother got the card, I signed it, and she mailed it to my job.

After I got out of the hospital, I was still in a crisis and in a lot of pain. The doctor suggested I stay home to recuperate. I got out of the hospital and was at home for a month and a week.

When I got back to my job, everyone welcomed me back. I met a lot of new people. I also got the opportunity to meet the three employees who had donated some of their sick days to me. I went to them and thanked them personally. I was shocked that three people who did not know me had donated some of their days to me. I will forever be indebted to them. All three of them are still a significant part of my life. I am thankful there are people who care for others and are willing to help a stranger in need. I wish I were able to be a blood donor, but I can't be, due to being sick. I wanted to be an organ donor, but I am not sure if I would be a great candidate. I always encourage all my family and friends to donate blood as much as possible so they can save someone's life. It is simple to donate blood and be the reason someone lives to see another day.

People started looking after me, making sure I was okay. I started educating people on sickle cell anemia. Some people had no clue what sickle cell was, because they had never heard of it. Others had heard of it but did not know much about it. My supervisor asked me to do a training session to educate my coworkers about sickle cell. I did a three-hour training, and it went well. My coworkers asked me a lot of questions about my disease, and I was able to answer them.

A few months later, I was in a tragic car accident. A drunk driver hit me. I was five minutes away from my home. I was stopped at a stop sign. I was just about to go, when I saw some car headlights coming toward me. The car was coming fast, and I was unable to move. The car slammed into me at sixty miles per hour. My car ended up spinning completely across the street into the bus stop lane. I was shaken up. I thought I was going to die.

When the car finally stopped, I was glad. I was confused, and I thought I should have been hurt a lot more than I was. My seat had folded up, and I was crushed in my seat. The windows were all broken. My car was crushed.

A man ran over to my car and said, "Are you okay?"

I said, "I think I am okay." I heard a loud hissing noise. I started climbing out the windshield.

The man said, "No, I think you should just wait for the police."

I said, "No, this car might blow up." I continued to climb out the windshield until I was out of my crushed car. The man followed me. We walked a few feet away from the car.

A lady and her little girl walked up to me. The lady asked me if I was okay, and I said, "I guess I am okay." Her little girl asked me if I needed to call someone. She handed me a phone. I called my sister and told her what had happened. She said she would be right there. I also called my friend who was my live-in roommate at the time. I also called a friend who lived across town. She said she was on her way.

Prior to my sister and my two friends getting to the scene of my horrific car accident, the man who'd hit me with his car, who was drunk and high on drugs, got out of his car and walked toward me and the three spectators standing near me. He walked up to me.

The police arrived as the man was standing in my face. The guy who'd seen the accident and was standing there with me walked over and explained to the police officers what had happened, because he was the witness. The officers came and pulled the drunk driver out of my face. He was drunk and high and belligerent. He was screaming and yelling at me.

There was a young white girl there who was about my age. She told the police she had been chasing the drunk driver because he had just hit her a few blocks away and sped off. She said she had been chasing him so she could get his insurance information. "Wow, all this is my fault. I should not have been chasing him, and he would not have hit her," she said, pointing to me.

The drunk driver started yelling at her too. The officers arrested him and put him in a squad car. He scared me; I thought he was going to hit me. The police officers had to threaten the drunk driver as they were putting him in the squad car.

My friend arrived on the scene and was out of breath because she had run to where I was. She started yelling. I told her to calm down because

I was okay. She had hung up the phone and run three blocks from our apartment, and she ran up to me crying. She was upset. My sister pulled up about five minutes later. I was calm until my sister arrived. As soon as I saw my sister, I started crying. I became emotional.

The ambulance arrived a few minutes after my sister. They had me lie down on a gurney. I was feeling okay. My friend got into the ambulance with me. My sister followed the ambulance. My other friend arrived about thirty minutes later. She ran over and hugged me. Just a few weeks before, she had lost a close family member who was hit in her car by a drunk driver. Crying, she said, "I just lost a family member. I do not want to lose my friend too." She was an emotional wreck. I tried to calm her down by reassuring her that I was not going to die and was going to be okay. It took a while for her to calm down.

I was in a lot of pain; my butt and my back were throbbing. I did not know I was in as much pain as I was in. The doctor noticed I was in so much pain that I could barely stand. The doctor said, "You will be really sore in the morning. You will be hurting for a few weeks." He sent me home with some strong pain medicines. He suggested I stay home for about a month.

I once again was worried about my job because I was still new, and besides, I had just been in a major crisis only two months ago. I called my supervisor and explained that I had just gotten hit by a drunk driver. She said, "Wow, you are having some bad luck, young lady. If you didn't have bad luck, you probably would not have any luck at all. I will solicit some more days for you from some more of our employees."

I said, "No, I do not need any more days; do not worry about me. I will be okay."

She said, "People at our job love to help one another. I have an idea. You can take the month off, and you can work in the twilight program and assist the night teachers until you work off all your days you took."

I liked that idea. No one would have to give up any of their days for me.

Due to the car accident, my body was in so much pain that it caused me to go into a crisis. I ended up being home for two months instead of one month. I ended up having to go back to the hospital, and I was admitted and was there for a month.

I felt bad because I had just started my new job and had not been there long at all. However, when a person has sickle cell, life can be unpredictable. Crises come when they want to. There is no warning that a crisis will come. They come like a thief in the night. I wish I had some control over them, but unfortunately, I do not.

CHAPTER 10

Finding Love

I was twenty-seven years old and had been at my job for three years. I had gotten a promotion, and I was now a teacher with my own class. I had been in my new role for three years and was happy. I had the job I had always wanted. However, there was one key element missing from my life: I did not have a boyfriend. I was single and had been for the past five years. My life was too busy, and I had no time for a relationship. I was working, going to school, and assisting my mother when she needed me. I was not able to add a man to the mix. But I decided to go against my own better judgment. I let a man into my life.

My sister called me and said, "I gave someone your number."

I was driving, so I paused. I said, "Okay, who did you give my number to?"

She laughed and said, "Oh, my boyfriend's brother."

"Who is your boyfriend's brother?"

"You know my boyfriend's brother."

I laughed. I remembered him. I had met him six years prior. He was cute, but he was not my type. He was a little too shy for me.

She said, "He just got to town, and he asked about you. He asked if you were dating or if you were in a serious relationship. My nephew was in the car, and he had to chime in. He said, 'My auntie is single.' He just moved back to town. I told him you were single, and I gave him your number."

I said, "Girl, why did you do that? You should have called me first."

She said, "Just be his friend. He could use a friend right now."

I said okay, and then we hung up.

When I got home, I checked my voice mail messages. He'd left me a message: "Hello. I called you to see how you have been doing. I just moved back to town, and I just wanted to know how things were going with you. You can give me a call back if you like." He'd left his number.

I hesitated before I decided to call him. I waited a couple of hours, and then I called him. I was a little nervous to call him at first. I was a little uncomfortable because I had not ever talked to him on the phone. I took a deep breath and then dialed his number. He answered, and we started a conversation. We talked for a few hours, and then we hung up. He asked me to come see him the next day. He was easy to talk to.

I went to see him the next day when I got off work. When I got to his house, he was sitting in the living room, watching TV. He opened his arms as if he wanted a hug. I extended my hand for a handshake. I do not like to hug people I do not know. I'd met him six years before, but I still really did not know him.

I stayed at his house for a few hours, and then I left. I lived ten minutes from him, and by the time I got home, he had left a message on my answering machine to call him. I smiled. I was flattered because I knew he liked me. I called him, and we talked for a couple of hours. Then I hung up so I could go to work.

We started seeing each other every day over the next couple of months. We were spending a lot of time together. We went to the park and walked around, just talking and getting to know each other. We were together either in person or on the phone.

One day I asked him if he knew what sickle cell anemia was. He looked at me and smiled. He said, "I've heard of it before, but I do not know what it is. I heard about it when I was in high school."

I asked him what he knew about sickle cell.

He said, "I know it is a blood disease, and mainly black people get it."

I smiled because he was correct, but there was a lot more to it than that. I proceeded to explain to him what it was. I told him, "If you want to run now, I will understand, and I will not be mad or hold it against you."

He laughed and said, "I'm not going to run. I'm here for the long haul."

I smiled.

I was in school, and he would help me with my homework. I explained to him that I had a terribly busy life and would not have a whole lot of time to be with him.

He laughed and said, "I'm a patient person. I'm willing to wait."

I told him, "No man makes it with me for longer than six months."

He smiled and said, "I will wait six years if I have to."

I told him, "My family is really an important part of my life."

He said, "Family is important to me too."

I decided to introduce him to my mother and my younger sister. My mother was shocked because I did not ever bring guys to meet her. She said, "You must like him." I blushed. She said it in front of him. He smiled at me.

My little sister said, "He is cute."

He smiled again. He was cute, but I did not like guys with braids. Not only did he have braids, but his braids were long.

A few days later, he called me on the phone. He asked me to come over, and I went over to see him. When I got there, he asked me to take down his braids. I said, "Why do you want me to take down your braids?"

He said, "I'm cutting my hair."

I asked him why.

He said, "I'm cutting my braids for two reasons. The first reason is because I know you do not like guys who have braids. The second reason is because I can get a job if I have a nice short haircut."

I stopped taking down his hair, looked at him, and said, "No, do not cut your hair for me."

He said, "Well, I am cutting it for you and so I can get a job."

I continued to take down his hair. After I was done, he asked me to take him to the barbershop. So I dropped him off at the barbershop. When I came back, he was sitting in the shop, waiting on me. He looked like a different person. I loved his short haircut. He was cute. I was flattered that he would cut his hair for me.

We officially started dating a few weeks later. We were inseparable from that moment on. I decided I would ask him if he wanted to move in with me, because he was always at my place anyway. He was at my place, and we were sitting in the living room. I looked at him and said, "You might as well move in here, because you are always over here anyway."

He laughed. "Yes, I can do that. You are right; I am always over here anyway. It is like I already live here anyway."

My boyfriend had been living with me for about two months, when I went into a crisis. I woke up early in the morning with chest pains. My lower back was throbbing. He was asleep. I yelled, "Wake up! I am in a crisis! I need you to take me to the emergency room."

He got up. He put on his clothes. What he did next blew my mind. He walked over to the dresser and grabbed his pack of cigarettes. He grabbed his lighter. He lit his cigarette right there in our apartment. I yelled, "Wayne, what the hell are you doing?"

He looked at me strangely and said, "Oh, my bad. I am sorry, babe. I am just so nervous."

I got dressed, and we walked downstairs to the car. He drove me to the emergency room. He was nervous. He kept going outside and taking five-minute smoke breaks until they put me in a room. I could tell he was nervous. He kept asking me over and over if I was okay. I was in so much pain, but I had to reassure him I was okay. But I was not okay.

Once they put me in my room, they had to start an IV on me. I was crying because I hate IVs. He saw the sadness in my eyes. He held my hand. He was patient with me. He looked sad because he hated to see me in pain.

When I got out of the hospital, I was unable to work for a few days. He took exceptionally good care of me. He had never had a girlfriend who had sickle cell anemia. He was learning as our relationship progressed.

CHAPTER 11

Surprises

My boyfriend and I had been together for about two months, when I got the surprise of my life. I was working, and I started having lower back pain and pelvic pain daily. My little sister said, "You are probably pregnant."

I said, "Girl, I'm not pregnant." My mind started wondering, and thoughts started racing through my head. *Could my sister be right? Am I pregnant?*

When I got home, my boyfriend was at work. I went to the local pharmacy and picked up two pregnancy tests. I went back home. I was nervous. I paced back and forth.

I was possibly going to have a baby. I was possibly going to be a mom. I was bombarded with many mixed emotions all at once. I was happy, sad, mad, glad, and confused all at the same time. I was concerned that I had sickle cell and about how it might affect me, and my unborn child was not at the top of my priority list, but I was excited about becoming a mama.

I was excited and decided to go take one of the tests while I was home alone. I went to the bathroom. I peed on the stick and walked out of the bathroom for a few minutes while the test was being conducted. I walked back into the bathroom, and the stick was a faint light blue. I was shocked because it showed I was pregnant. I sat there just waiting for my boyfriend to come home.

When he got home, I was excited. I said, "I have something to show you." I walked into the bathroom and grabbed the pregnancy test, and the line was still a faint blue color on the stick.

He looked at the stick and then at me. "You're pregnant? Is that right?"

I looked at him and said, "Yes, it's right. Look—it is blue." He still was in disbelief. I told him, "I bought two pregnancy tests."

He said, "You did?"

I said, "Yes, we can take another one."

I went and took the second pregnancy test. I walked out of the bathroom and sat on the couch next to him. He was smiling, but I could tell he was nervous. I told him everything was going to be okay. We talked for a few minutes, and then I walked into the bathroom to get the result of the second pregnancy test. It was blue just like the first one, but it was not faint at all. He looked at me. I looked at him. We both smiled. We were having a baby.

I immediately walked over and picked up my phone and dialed my mother's number. My mother answered. She said, "Hey, Klee, how are you doing?"

I said, "Mama, I'm doing fairly good. How are you doing, Mom?"

She said, "I'm doing fairly good."

I said, "Mom, there is something I need to tell you."

"Okay."

"Mama, I am pregnant."

She said, "Oh, that's good. Congratulations."

I said, "Thank you, Mom." I asked her not to tell anyone, because I wanted to wait a while before I shared the news with anyone else. We hung up.

I was about four months pregnant when I started having complications. I had a doctor's appointment for an ultrasound. I was going to see the sex of my unborn child. One of my older sisters decided to meet up with me at the hospital for my ultrasound appointment. Prior to my appointment, I was instructed by the hospital to drink a lot of water prior to my visit. I drank a lot of water, but I needed to go to the bathroom. When I got to my appointment, I told the nurse I needed to use the bathroom.

She said, "Oh, you can go use the bathroom."

I felt much better after I used the bathroom. My sister was there waiting in the waiting room. She walked up to me and hugged me. She rubbed my stomach. We sat back down and waited for my name to be called. We were talking, when a nurse came out and tried to call my name. She pronounced it incorrectly. I laughed because I was used to people mispronouncing my name. I corrected her, as I usually do. She apologized and walked me and my sister to the back and took us into a room. I was given a gown to change into. I left my sister in the room, and I went and changed into the gown the nurse had handed me. I walked back into the room, where my sister was waiting for me.

The nurse reentered the room with an ultrasound machine. She explained to me what she was going to do. She put some jelly-like gel on my stomach. The gel was extremely cold. She grabbed what is known as a wand, with a piece of plastic over it. She rolled it back and forth across my stomach. I was looking at the screen, and so was my sister. The nurse suddenly changed her facial expression. She was smiling at first, but then her whole disposition changed in a single second. She looked scared. She stopped the test. She said, "I need you to go use the restroom again, because I see a lot of water. Your bladder needs to be empty for this test."

I looked at her as if she were crazy. "I'm confused. First, you guys told me I had to drink a lot of water because I needed a full bladder for this test."

She said, "Yes, we did say that, but now I need for your bladder to be empty."

I was frustrated. I got up and went to use the bathroom. Before I went to the bathroom, she handed me some paper towels so I could wipe the gel off my stomach.

After I came out of the bathroom, I lay back down so she could finish my procedure. She restarted my test. Then she stopped in the middle of it and excused herself for a few minutes. She was gone for about five minutes, but it seemed more like an hour.

My sister said, "I think something is wrong."

I looked at her. "Why do you think something is wrong?"

She said, "The way that nurse is acting."

The nurse walked back into the room. She said, "I can't finish the procedure. You will have to go see your primary care doctor." She started wiping the cold gel off my stomach.

My sister said, "Is there something wrong?"

She said, "No, ma'am, there is not anything wrong. I just am unable to continue the test here in my department. However, her primary care doctor will have to explain to her what is going on. You can get dressed now. Please go call your primary doctor and make an appointment immediately."

She left, and I got dressed. My sister said, "There is something wrong."

My sister and I left. We were walking to my car, and my sister hugged me. I started crying. My sister said, "Do not worry; God has you. You will be okay."

I watched my sister walk away. I continued to cry. I cried for about ten minutes. I decided to call my mom because she always knew what to say to make me feel better. I dialed my mom's number. When my mom answered, I started crying uncontrollably.

My mom said, "What is wrong?" I was too upset to talk. My mama told me to stop crying. "I need for you to calm down. I cannot help you if you do not tell me what is going on."

I calmed myself down. I explained to her what had just happened at my appointment.

She said, "The nurse did not say anything was wrong. Just call and make an appointment with your doctor." She reassured me that I was going to be fine. I hung up the phone.

I was still sad. I had to call my boyfriend. I knew he was at work, but I needed him to know what I was going through. I called, but he was busy, so I told the lady on the phone that it was an emergency and to please have him call me as soon as possible. Ten minutes later, my phone rang, it was him. I was stressed as well as emotional. I was crying.

He said, "What is wrong?"

I told him what had happened at my doctor's appointment.

He said, "Both you and our baby are going to be fine. Call your doctor, and make the appointment."

We hung up. I just sat in my car crying. I was scared I was going to lose my son. I had decided to name him Keon.

I called my doctor, and they scheduled me an appointment for the next day. I wanted my boyfriend to go with me, but he had to work. I went by myself. If I had known the news the doctor was going to give me, I would have taken someone with me.

I got to the doctor's office at ten thirty, and my appointment was at 11:00 a.m. I waited a few minutes, and then they called me to the back. The nurse weighed me. She looked at me funny. She said, "Wow, you sure are losing a lot of weight. Most women usually gain weight." I had lost about thirty pounds.

She checked my blood pressure. She walked me to a room. She asked me some general questions. She said, "The doctor will be in shortly." She left.

My doctor walked into the room. He said, "How are you doing today?"

I looked at him strangely. I said, "Well, I thought I was doing okay, until I was told to come here today."

He smiled. He said, "How have you been feeling lately?"

I said, "Well, I have been vomiting a whole lot. I am always feeling sick."

He said, "Well, I have some bad news."

My eyes got big. What he said next blew my mind.

He said, "You have cervical cancer."

I sat up straight on the patient bed. "I have what?"

He said, "I'm sorry, but you have cervical cancer in the second stage." I began crying. He said, "Please do not cry."

I looked at him. How did he expect me not to cry, when he'd just told me that I had cervical cancer and that it was already in the second stage?

He said, "You can still carry the baby, but you may possibly lose him." I cried even more. He said, "We will do all we can to try to help you carry the baby to full term."

I said, "So what about the cancer? How do you get it out?"

He said, "After your baby is born, we will do a general procedure in the hospital called a leap procedure. We will freeze all the cancer cells off. It is a quick and simple procedure. Do not worry about that right now; just focus on having a healthy baby boy."

I said, "It's a boy? How do you know?"

He said, "I saw it on the ultrasound."

I smiled. I always had wanted a son.

He said, "Congratulations on having a son. I am sorry I had to be the bearer of bad news." He asked if I had any questions.

I said, "Yes, if I end up losing my baby, when will they do the leap procedure?"

He said, "Do not worry about that right now. Please just focus on giving birth to a healthy baby boy." He smiled at me, and I managed to smile back. He said, "I noticed that you are losing a lot of weight. Do you know why you are losing a lot of weight?"

I looked at him and said, "I do not know." But I was not being honest. I had stopped eating food almost three weeks prior to my appointment. My boyfriend and my mama were not aware that I had stopped eating food. I did not want to tell the doctor that I was basically starving myself because it was too painful to eat and throw up. I should have been honest with the doctor and my family. I was not aware that my little secret was making matters worse.

I ended up going into preterm labor a month and a half later. I was at home, and I started feeling extreme pain in my lower back. I told my boyfriend to take me to the emergency room. He rushed me to the emergency room. They took me right back. They prepped me to give birth. They put me in a birthing bed. The bed was uncomfortable.

The doctor walked into the room. He introduced himself. He was friendly, and he seemed to be empathetic toward my situation. He said, "We will have to take your baby."

I sat up in the bed with tears in my eyes. My boyfriend walked over to me and hugged me. He held my hand.

The doctor said, "Okay, you will have to push him out."

I said, "No, I cannot do that."

My boyfriend said, "Babe, you have to."

I started crying. The doctor said, "When you push him out, he will not be alive." He put his stethoscope on and walked near me. He said, "You guys can listen to his heartbeat before you push him out."

I just started crying. I was not strong enough to listen to my baby's heartbeat. My boyfriend listened to his heartbeat. After my boyfriend listened to his heartbeat, the doctor prepped me by telling me how to push. I pushed for about fifteen minutes, and then my son came out. He was so tiny. He was half a pound and seventeen inches. He looked like a doll. He looked sad. I cried after I pushed him out.

My boyfriend was lying on the floor in the fetal position, crying like a baby. The doctor even had tears in his eyes. We were all sad.

A nurse walked into the room. She introduced herself. She said, "Would you like to look at your son?"

I said no at first. I needed to hear what she said next. She said, "If I were you, I would look at him and hold him, because once they take him to the morgue, he will be gone. You do not want to ever regret not knowing who or what he looked like. I will take your son and clean him up and dress him and bring him back. May I ask what his name is?"

I looked at my boyfriend and started crying harder. I said, "His name is Keon."

She smiled. She took my son and walked out of the room. My boyfriend got off the floor, got into my hospital bed, and lay right next to me.

My best friend walked into the hospital. She hugged me and said, "I feel bad for you, girl. Do not worry, girl; you two will have more children." She sat down in a chair next to my bed.

The nurse walked in with my deceased son. He looked different with clothes and a hat on. She had him in a small wicker basket. She handed it to me. I was holding him, when my best friend stood up and looked at him. She said, "Wow, girl, he looks just like you."

I looked at him, and he did look just like me. She reached out her hand to hold him. I handed her the basket. She picked him up and held him. She had tears in her eyes. She held him for a long time.

I said, "Hey, girl, let me hold him for a while."

She placed him back in the basket. She handed him to me. I held him for a while. Then my boyfriend held him for a while. My friend left. A nurse came in later and asked if I wanted to donate my son to science. I said, "No, I do not want to donate my son to science." She left.

I wanted to bury my son, but we did not have the money to bury him, so I cremated him instead. Walking into a funeral home to pick out an urn for our son was the most difficult thing we had to do. We had a hard time picking an urn for our son, but God gave us the strength we needed to do what we had to do.

CHAPTER 12

More Loss

Losing my son Keon was a life-changing event that affected my life in many ways. My boyfriend and I were sad. Not only had we lost our son, but I still had cervical cancer. I got my leap procedure six weeks later. My mama went with me and was there while I got my procedure done. It was a quick forty-five-minute surgery that was simple.

Four months later, I was pregnant again with my second son. I was excited and scared. I'd lost one son and was scared I might lose my second son too. My boyfriend was excited. I did not want to tell anyone but my mom. I did not want to tell anyone in case I miscarried again.

I called and told my mom. She was happy and worried at the same time. She wanted to be a grandmother but not if it put her child's life in jeopardy. I understood how my mom felt about me, because I was her child.

I was four months along, when I got into an argument with my boyfriend. I was yelling at him, and he was calm. He did not want to argue with me, because I was pregnant and considered high risk. I do not even remember what we were arguing about that day. My boyfriend called his brother, and then he left. After he left, I got a boost of energy from nowhere. I felt like Wonder Woman or some other superhero. I got up and cleaned my whole house. I had not ever had that much energy while I was pregnant before.

I decided to call my sister and invited her and her four children over to my place. I made lunch for all of us. My sister and I then sat around the pool, watching her children play in the water.

My boyfriend came into the pool area. He said, "You know you better not get in that pool."

I looked at him and said, "I'm a grown-ass woman; I can do what I want to do. You are not my daddy or my husband."

He left again with his brother. I was upset. I was going to show his ass that I was grown. I got in the pool. I knew better than to get into a pool. I got in for about fifteen minutes.

My sister said, "You'd better get out of that pool. You might go into a crisis."

I knew my sister was right, so I got out of the pool. I did not think I would go into a crisis, because it was hot outside.

My sister and her children had been gone for hours prior to my boyfriend coming home. I was still upset when he came through the door. He tried to talk to me, but I just ignored him. He made himself some food, and then he went into our bedroom and lay down. I decided to be defiant and sleep in the living room. I walked into our bedroom, snatched my pillow and blanket off the bed, and left to sleep on the couch. As I was walking out of the room, he said, "You do not have to sleep on the couch." I slammed the door and ignored him.

I was sleeping on the couch, when I was awakened by a painful leg crisis. I was in so much pain I yelled for my boyfriend. He came running into the living room. He said, "Babe, what is wrong?"

I said, "I'm in a crisis; my left leg is in a lot of pain."

He said, "Okay, I'm going to get dressed, and then I'll bring you some clothes to put on." He came back and assisted me down the stairs and into the car.

On the way to the hospital, I started crying. He looked at me and said, "Babe, why are you crying?"

I said, "It's my fault. I got in the swimming pool after you told me not to."

He stopped the car and looked at me with an angry look. "Babe, I told you not to do that."

I said, "I know. I was angry with you."

He looked at me. He said, "Babe, you are so stubborn. But do not worry; the baby will be okay."

We arrived at the hospital in about ten minutes. He took me to the emergency department. They immediately sent me over to labor and delivery. When I got to the labor and delivery department, they checked me out. Then they sent me back to the emergency room because I was in a crisis. They said they had to try to get me out of the crisis. They put me in a room.

The doctor came into the room. She said, "What happened? How did you go into a crisis? Do you typically have a crisis in the summertime?"

I said, "I'm in a crisis. Crises just come when they want to; I have no control over when or why they come. Like I said, I can go into a crisis at any time."

My boyfriend said, "Excuse me, but what can you do for her while she is in a crisis?"

The doctor said, "Sir, we will do all we can to try to save your baby, but we have to get her out of the crisis first. We will have to give you morphine. Once we give you morphine, your unborn baby may possibly die due to the morphine being such a strong drug."

I started crying. My boyfriend hugged me. The doctor walked out of the room.

I said, "This is all my fault. I should not have gotten in that pool."

My boyfriend said, "Who knows? Maybe you were just going to have a crisis anyway. Stop blaming yourself." He kissed me.

I started crying harder. I said, "If I lose this baby, I will just feel so bad. Can you please tell them to save our baby instead of me?"

He said, "Are you crazy? I want the baby, but I need you. We can always have another baby. I'm gonna call your mama." He picked up the hospital phone and dialed my mom's number. I heard my mama say hello. He said, "She's in a crisis. They say she might lose the baby when they give her morphine. She wants them to save the baby and not herself."

My mama must have gotten angry, because he handed me the phone. I said, "Hello."

My mama said, "Hello. I love you and your unborn son, but I have known you a lot longer. I do not even know him. You are my baby. You take that morphine so they can get you out of that crisis." I started crying again. My mama said, "You will be okay. You and your boyfriend can have more children later. I love you. I will not lose my child just so I can be a grandmother." We hung up. I cried more.

A nurse walked into the room with all the equipment she needed for my IV. She introduced herself. She said, "Okay, I will be giving you an IV and fluids so you can feel better." I hated IVs, but the pain was unbearable.

Once the morphine kicked in, I felt a little better.

I was in the hospital for three weeks because it was a bad leg crisis. The crisis was a difficult one that was hard to get rid of. I ended up going into preterm labor, and my second son, Kenneth, was born at sixteen weeks. He slid right out of me into the bed. He was born alive. However, he only took a few short breaths, and then he died.

I ended up being sent back home because the hospital was unable to get me out of the crisis. They said they had done all they possibly could. I was in the crisis for three weeks after I was released. I'd lost my second son, and I was hurt and devastated.

After I got out of the hospital, I went home and lay in my bed for three weeks until I was completely well. I went back to work so I could keep my mind off losing my second son.

My family and close friends told me to give up because they were tired of seeing me suffering and hurt. They suggested we just adopt a baby instead. My mama was adamant about my not needing to get pregnant again. I had a lot of respect for my mom and my family and friends, but I was not going to give up; I was going to keep trying until I was able to have a baby. It was now a goal of mine, and I was on a mission. My boyfriend and I decided to wait a year before we tried again. I got on birth control in the meantime.

CHAPTER 13

New Life

A year later, I was pregnant for the third time with my son Jayce. I was at work one day, and I started feeling sick. I walked to the bathroom, and I threw up everywhere. I did not think I might be pregnant. I had just gotten off birth-control pills only six months earlier.

I walked to my car and sat there for my whole lunch break. I called my boyfriend and told him I felt sick. He said, "Babe, maybe it was something you ate."

I said, "You might be right." However, it seemed it was more than something I had eaten. We hung up.

I had a feeling I might be pregnant, but I was not sure. I went back into my classroom. My coteacher said, "Are you okay? You look a little pale."

I smiled and said, "I'm okay. I am just a little tired. I did not get much sleep."

I left work, and I went by the pharmacy and got two pregnancy tests. I was not feeling well at all. The smell of the air conditioner was even bothering me. Everything I ate made me sick.

I got home, and my boyfriend was at work. I took one of the pregnancy tests. I went into the living room and sat on the couch while I waited for my test result. I then walked into the restroom and looked at my result, and it was positive. I was happy.

I wanted to call my mama to share my good news, but I did not because I knew how she and my other family and friends felt about my getting pregnant. They all wished I would just adopt a baby or not have any more children, period. I decided at that moment to keep my secret for a little while. I was close to my mama, and keeping the secret was going to be difficult. I always talked to my mama when I needed some great advice.

When my boyfriend arrived home, I was making dinner. He walked in and hugged and kissed me. He said, "Babe, why are you so happy?"

I walked into the bathroom and grabbed the first pregnancy test. I handed it to him.

He smiled. "Babe, is this real?" I nodded, and he said, "Wow."

I said, "I knew I was pregnant. I have another pregnancy test; I can take it."

He said, "No, I believe you, babe. But if you want to be sure, you can go take the other test."

I said, "I believe I am pregnant, but it does not hurt to take it again and get the same result."

I went into the restroom and took the second test. I went into the living room and talked to my boyfriend while we waited for the result. I walked back into the restroom, and the stick was blue. I walked into the living room and showed him the blue lines on the pregnancy test.

He smiled. "I'm so happy."

I said, "I do not want anyone to know."

He said, "Okay, but in a few months, they will find out. How are you feeling?"

I said, "I'm feeling okay. I am just a little nervous. I am a little afraid because we already lost two of our sons before."

He said, "Babe, that is in the past. God will keep this baby. We will be fine."

I had a doctor's appointment, and my doctor explained to me that I had what was known as an incompetent cervix, which basically meant I had a hard time holding babies in full term. He also said I would have to get a cerclage when I was four months pregnant.

I looked at him. "What is a cerclage? How do you do the procedure?"

He smiled. "The proper name is cervical cerclage, which is a procedure that women with an incompetent cervix usually have to have so they can carry their baby to full term. It is only done once a woman reaches four months and above. It is a simple surgery, and a woman is usually in and out of the hospital that same day." My eyes got big. He said, "It is a really painless surgery and is quite simple and very quick. Trust me: you and your unborn baby will be fine."

He asked his nurse to go get him the ultrasound machine. The nurse left the room and came back into the room with the device. He put the cold gel on my stomach. He put the plastic on the wand. He rolled the wand back and forth across my stomach and said, "I will be listening and looking for the baby's heartbeat." He smiled. He let me hear my baby's heartbeat and showed my baby's heart beating on the ultrasound machine. He smiled again and said, "Look—you have a healthy baby." He then said, "You may get dressed. After you are done getting dressed, please go see my nurse so you can schedule your appointment for your cerclage procedure."

I was happy. I made my appointment for my cerclage procedure. I left the hospital feeling great.

Two weeks before the four-month mark, I decided to tell my supervisor at my job that I was pregnant. I walked into my supervisor's office. I told him I needed to speak with him. He asked me to close the door and sit down in a chair. He said, "How can I help you?"

I smiled and said, "I just found out that I'm almost four months pregnant."

He started clapping his hands and said congratulations.

I said, "Thank you!"

What he said next was mind-blowing. He said, "I think you need to be placed on bed rest because you are a high-risk pregnant woman. I think you would be much safer at home." He got on his computer and printed out a form. He handed me the form. "Take this to your doctor, and ask him to place you on bed rest. This is the part they will require me to complete. However, it will be already done."

I said, "Thank you. I would prefer that you not tell any of my coworkers. I will tell them when I am ready." I did not like my supervisor, and the feeling was mutual. But in that moment, I saw him in a different light. Still, I did not trust him. I usually took a witness into his office with me when I went to talk with him.

He said, "Please relax, and take it easy; you have a baby to take care of."

I looked at him. I said, "Are you okay?"

He said, "Please just be careful because I do not want you to lose your baby, because you have lost two babies already."

I said, "I will be careful, and thank you." I left his office. I did not go back to work until I had my son.

On the day of my cerclage procedure, I was nervous. My surgery was scheduled for 7:00 p.m. I walked into the hospital not knowing exactly what to expect. I prayed before I went into surgery. They told me to go change into a hospital gown. I changed into the garment and walked back into the room they had me waiting in. A nurse came and explained what was going to happen during the procedure.

Before the procedure, I'd decided I had to tell my mother I was pregnant. I was nervous, but I had to tell her. I decided to go to her house to tell her in person. I went downstairs to my mom's apartment, which was in the same complex. My mother answered the door. She said, "Hey, how are you doing?" Tears filled my eyes. My mama said, "What is wrong?"

I said, "Mom, I'm pregnant."

My mama looked at me. She smiled. "Oh, is that it?"

I nodded. "I know you did not want me to have any more children."

She smiled. "No, I said I was tired of you suffering. I understand that you want to be a mom. But I am your mom, and I just want my child to be okay." She hugged me. "How many months are you?"

"I will be four months in two weeks. I must get a cerclage."

My mama looked at me funny.

I said, "They said I have an incompetent cervix, which means I have a hard time holding babies. The cerclage is one big stitch that they place over my uterus so the baby has no way to get out, and he will stay in."

My mom said, "Wow, you are having another boy."

I smiled. "Yes, the third time is the charm, right? Mom, you can tell my siblings."

They rolled my hospital bed into the surgery room. When I got into the surgery room, I was scared. The surgeon asked me if I understood how the procedure worked. I said, "Yes, the nurse explained it to me."

He said, "Okay, I would like to explain it to you too. You will be awake while we do the procedure. You will have a large sheet over your stomach, and you will be unable to see us doing the cerclage. You will not be able to see us sewing the stitch that will be the actual cerclage. You will be numb and unable to feel it while we are doing the procedure, but you may be in a lot of pain afterward, while you are recovering. We are going to give you some numbing medicine, and then we will start the procedure after we feel that you are numb."

After five or ten minutes, I was numb. A nurse said, "We will be starting in a few minutes. Please try to think of a happy place that will keep you calm and distract you while we are doing the procedure."

I immediately started thinking about my youngest niece. I thought about taking her to the park, as I did from time to time. I had a hard time not looking at them stitching me up. Even though I could not feel it, it still creeped me out to see the needle and thread going back and forth as they stitched my uterus.

The procedure was quick, and I was sent to the recovery room. When they took me to the recovery room, I was still numb. However, after about two hours, the numbing medicine wore off. I was in so much pain. I kept calling the nurse. She explained to me that they could not give me any heavy drugs, such as narcotics, because I was pregnant. All they could give me was Tylenol because it was the only medicine they allowed pregnant women. My stomach felt as if someone were twisting it, like wringing out a shirt. I was in so much pain that I was crying. My nurse felt bad for me. She kept coming to check on me.

The last time she came, she said, "Well, I'm heading home. I know you will be better soon. Good luck to you and your baby."

I managed a weak smile. I said, "Thank you. I appreciate you for being so nice." She left. I had to spend the night at the hospital.

I felt much better the next day. My boyfriend came to the hospital to pick me up, and then he took me home. I was placed on bed rest for the next four months. It was hard to just lie in bed all day and only be allowed to go make something to eat or use the restroom. I had to lie down most of the day.

Prior to having the surgery, I was going to name my son Elijah. I wanted him to have a biblical name. However, as I was asleep on my couch one day, something said, "Wake up."

I woke up and turned on the TV, and I saw credits rolling. The name Jace Wright went across the screen. I sat straight up. I said, "Wow, I like that name." I touched my stomach, and I said, "Your name will be Jace."

I went back and forth with the spelling of the name. I spelled it Jaice, Jace, and then, finally, Jayce. My mom's name was Joyce. I changed the *o* to an *a*, and I had Jayce. He was going to be named after my mom.

I called my mother immediately. I told her I'd changed my son's name. I explained to my mama how I'd gotten his name and why I spelled it the way I did. She loved the name and how I spelled it, and the fact that he was named after her was cool.

One of my older sisters brought me over a lot of movies. My friend brought me some paperwork I could do at home. My mama would call me all day long to check up on me and Jayce.

My boyfriend and I had broken up. He was no longer in my apartment with me. We went through some things, and I decided to put him out because I was not going to risk losing my son. I had already lost two of my sons. I refused to lose Jayce. My boyfriend was stressing me out, and I knew if I was stressed out, I might lose my baby. I had lost my first son, Keon, at five months and my second son, Kenneth, at four months. I was now almost five months along with my son Jayce. I had to be calm and stress free if I wanted to deliver a full-term baby.

Even though my boyfriend and I were no longer together, he called to check up on me every other day. We were civil with each other. I kept our conversations short and quick. I would give him updates about how our baby and I were doing. I told him I was going to have my baby shower. He asked me if he could come. I told him no because I did not want him there. He got mad. We argued, and then I hung up on him. He kept calling back, but I refused to answer the phone.

I had my baby shower that Saturday at my friend's sister's clubhouse at her apartment. My baby shower was nice. I was pleased with how it turned out. A lot more people than I expected showed up. I got a lot of nice things. People bought me a lot of stuff. I had three cars full of stuff to take back to my apartment. I was excited and felt blessed.

I had two more months until Jayce was going to be born. However, my son had other plans. I went into preterm labor a week after my baby shower. It was a Thursday night, and I started having cramps. My brother took me to the emergency room. He and I sat in that hospital for six long hours before they sent me home.

My brother went to my mom's house, and I went upstairs to my apartment. I went to go use the bathroom before going to sleep. I used the bathroom, and I went and lay down. A minute later, I had to use the bathroom again. I lay down again, and my phone rang. It was my boyfriend. He was calling to check up on me. I told him I'd just gotten back from the emergency room and was tired. I told him to call me tomorrow.

After I hung up, I went to the bathroom again. I became worried. I called my mom.

She said, "What is wrong?"

I said, "Mom, I keep having to go to the restroom every few minutes."

She said, "It sounds like your water bag is leaking. You'd better get to the hospital."

I said, "Okay, Mama. I will come get the keys to the van."

I walked downstairs to my mom's apartment, and she opened the door and handed me the key. My brother was on the couch, knocked out. My mama said, "I can wake your brother up."

I said, "No, I can drive myself." I got in the van and drove myself to the hospital.

I went to the labor and delivery ward. I knew I was in labor. A nurse walked up to me and said, "You and a young man just left here about twenty minutes ago, right?"

I said, "Yes, ma'am. But I am back. I think my water bag is leaking."

She went and got a wheelchair and rolled me to a room. They had me take off my clothes and change into a hospital gown. They called the anesthesiologist so they could give me an epidural. I got the epidural that night. However, my son did not come.

Two days later, they gave me another epidural, and my son still did not come.

Two days after that, they gave me another epidural. They also pulled my cerclage stich out, hoping my son would come right after they took it out. But no, he had to wait twelve hours later to make his grand entrance. The epidural wore off in about four hours. I had to suffer for eight hours. My two older sisters were with me at the hospital the entire time. One of my sisters attempted to call my boyfriend but was unable to get a hold of him.

At about one o'clock in the afternoon, I started feeling some big contractions. My chest started feeling funny. A nurse came in to check me, and I said, "I feel funny."

She called an EKG technician. The technician came and did an EKG on me. She looked at me funny and said, "I know you are not having a heart attack. You are too young."

I looked at her and said, "No, you are wrong, ma'am. A ten-year-old child can have a heart attack."

She did the test. When she left, she had a smirk on her face. My sisters were looking at me as if I were crazy. I wanted to be safe and not sorry.

A few hours later, my chest felt funny again. They did another EKG on me. They still did not find anything wrong with my chest.

An hour later, a nurse came to check my vitals, and she noticed my blood pressure was getting too high. She was concerned. They brought a machine in, and it screwed into my baby's head. It hurt. I was crying. The nurse said, "Your baby is in distress, and his blood pressure is up."

The doctor checked me and said I was dilated to ten centimeters.

It was seven o'clock that evening when they rolled me into the birthing room. The doctor said, "Okay, you will be giving birth in a few minutes." However, she was wrong, because those few minutes turned into an hour and eighteen minutes. I was in a lot of pain. She cut me with her scalpel, and I screamed. She said, "Oh, I forgot to deaden you." Then she deadened me. I yelled. She apologized. My son kept going down, but when they would attempt to grab him, he would go back up the birth canal. They mentioned suctioning him out, and my son stayed still, so they could get him out. My son was born at 8:18 p.m.

I was happy and excited to meet my son Jayce. He weighed three pounds and nine ounces and was nineteen inches long. A month before giving birth to my son, I'd had to get two steroid shots so my baby's lungs would develop much quicker. My son had weighed only one pound then.

Jayce was born at thirty-two weeks. He was so tiny he looked like a doll. When he came out, his cry sounded like that of a cat. I looked up to see if it was an actual cat in the delivery room. I said, "Wow, is there a cat in the room?"

The nurse laughed. She said, "No, that was your baby." I smiled.

They took my son to the NIC unit. He was little, but he was strong. He did not need a breathing machine, nor did he get jaundice, and he ate right away. Jayce had to stay in the hospital for three weeks before I was able to bring him home. He was five pounds when I was able to take him home. I was scared to take him home, because he was so small. I suffered from postpartum depression. I was worried because he was so tiny, and I did not want to hurt him. I did not feel as if I wanted to hurt him; I was just overwhelmed at first. I took my son home, and my mother taught me how to take care of Jayce.

I did not have a crisis at all while pregnant with Jayce. I think I did well when I was pregnant. I had an overall great pregnancy. I lost fifty pounds in several weeks due to not being able to hold down any food; however, I survived by eating limón chips and drinking Gatorade the entire time I was pregnant. I just ate and threw up right after I ate. I had to make sure my baby was getting the nutrients he needed to survive.

He was born a few weeks before Mother's Day. He was the greatest Mother's Day gift I ever got. He was my blessing from God. I thought I had loved before, but when I gave birth to my son, I felt a new love immediately. I hadn't known I was capable of loving someone like I love my son. When I pushed him out and laid eyes on him for the first time, I cried tears of joy. I was finally a mother, and I had a little human being who needed and depended on me. I was now responsible for him and was the one who had to take care of him and protect him. I was going to be the one who instilled his morals, values, and personal beliefs in him. He's still my favorite guy today. I loved watching him transition from a baby into a young man now.

CHAPTER 14

Road-Trip Crisis

When I was thirty-two years old, I had another difficult crisis. My son was one year old, and his dad and I had gotten back together. We were all preparing to take a road trip from California to Mississippi to see my boyfriend's mom. Although my boyfriend and I had been together for four years off and on, I had not met his mom yet. We wanted her to meet her grandson, Jayce. We were going to drive there and stop in Texas to see some of my family while on the way to Mississippi.

It took us three days to get to Mississippi. When we got there, I was very tired. I did not know why I was tired, because I had not driven at all. My boyfriend had driven the entire time. I had no energy at all. I did not tell my boyfriend I felt so exhausted.

We went to his grandmother's house, and everyone was there: his grandmother, his mother, aunties, uncles, and a lot of other family members. When we walked into Big Mama's house, his mother was sitting on the couch. She got up and hugged my boyfriend. He said, "Mom, this is my girlfriend and our son Jayce."

She hugged me and then held out her arms and grabbed Jayce. He went right to her. She walked away and went and introduced him to everyone. She was a proud grandma. She said, "Wow, he looks just like his daddy when he was little."

My boyfriend's mom told us that her mom was not feeling well. She said, "Big Mama may be too weak to get up and come into the living room. You guys will probably have to go into her room to see her." Boy, was she wrong, because Big Mama not only got up and walked down her hallway but was singing and dancing a jig. She walked down the hallway and hugged my boyfriend, and then she hugged me. She sat on the couch. My son's grandmother walked over to the couch and handed Jayce to Big Mama. She was smiling, and she looked happy. I could not even tell she was sick.

My boyfriend said, "Let's go get our stuff out of the car and take it out to my mother's house." I looked at my son. He said, "He will be okay; my mama will watch him. She does not mind watching her grandson."

We went and got the stuff out of the car. We took all our things into his mother's house, and then we went back to Big Mama's house.

I sat on the couch. I felt a little dizzy. My boyfriend asked me, "Babe, are you okay?"

I said, "I'm okay. I need some water."

He went and got me some water. I was sweating a lot. He said, "Are you sure you are okay?"

I said, "Yes, I'm just hot."

He said, "Okay, let me know if you need something."

The next day, they had a family gathering, and there were at least a hundred people there, all family and close friends. I met so many people that I do not remember who they all were. They cooked all kinds of food.

In the middle of the family gathering, I started to feel nauseated. I told my boyfriend I was not feeling well. I was feeling sick and so overwhelmed that I went to his mother's house. I took my son with me. My stepson and my niece went with me. When we got to my boyfriend's mom's house, I lay down on the couch. I took a nap.

I woke up two hours later in a deep sweat. My niece said, "Auntie, are you okay? You do not look well."

I said, "I'm okay. I am just a little hot." She turned the air conditioner on for me.

The next day, when I woke up, I was feeling nauseated. I told my boyfriend. He said, "Do you need to go to the hospital?"

I said, "No, I'll be okay." But I was lying because I was sick.

He took Jayce out to Big Mama's house. I was at his mama's house alone. I just lay on the couch and slept for a few hours. My sister came to my boyfriend's mother's house to check on me. She said, "You do not look good. How are you feeling?"

I lied and said, "I'm okay."

She said, "Well, you do not look okay. I'm going to get your boyfriend." She left.

My boyfriend, his mother, his aunt, and my sister all came to my boyfriend's mother's house. My boyfriend sat on the couch next to me. He said, "Your sister said you look sick. Babe, are you okay?"

I managed a smile. "I told you earlier that I was okay."

His aunt said, "Are you in any pain?"

I said, "Yes, my lower back is hurting."

She said, "I have a heating pad at home. I will go home and get it, and I will be right back." She left.

My boyfriend said, "We might need to go to the hospital if you get worse. I'm going back to Big Mama's house. If you are sure you are okay, I am going back outside." He left.

I was okay. I was just in the house, sleeping off and on. He kept coming in and out of his mom's house to check on me.

The next morning, when I got up, I felt horrible. I threw up in the bed my boyfriend, our son, and I were sleeping in. My boyfriend had me go lie down in the living room. I lay on the couch, and my boyfriend's mom asked me how I was doing. I said, "I'm not doing so good."

She told my boyfriend that he might need to take me to the hospital. My boyfriend and his brother disagreed about which hospital was the best to go to.

I said, "Please just take me to the nearest hospital."

My boyfriend took me to a hospital, which was fifteen minutes away. When we arrived there, a nurse walked out to the emergency room counter. She said, "May I help you two?"

My boyfriend said, "Yes, my girlfriend is in a crisis. She has sickle cell anemia."

She looked strange.

We waited a few minutes, and then they took me back to a room. They had me get undressed and put on a hospital gown. We were in there for a few minutes, when a doctor walked into the room. He introduced himself to me and my boyfriend. My boyfriend shook his hand and said, "Doc, do you know what sickle cell anemia is?"

The doctor smiled. He said, "I may know a little about it." Then he smiled again. "I honestly am remarkably familiar with sickle cell anemia. I studied the disease. I did not just read books about it; I made it my duty to learn all I could about the disease."

My boyfriend smiled. "Good. We came to the right hospital."

The doctor prescribed me morphine, IV fluids, and oxygen and also ran lots of tests on me.

The doctor came back to my room two hours later. He said, "How are you doing?"

I said, "I'm still in a lot of pain."

He said, "Okay, I will have the nurse give you more medicine. Your lab results came back. You were pregnant, but it looks like you miscarried the baby."

I looked at him funny. Then I looked at my boyfriend. He shrugged. We had not even been aware that I was pregnant. We were clueless.

The doctor said, "You will need a blood transfusion because your blood cell counts are extremely low. Do you have diabetes?"

I looked at him. "No, but I did have gestational diabetes twice before when I was pregnant with my first two sons."

He said, "Well, your sugar levels are way too high. We are going to treat you as if you have diabetes so we can get your sugar levels under control."

I said okay.

He said, "You will have to be admitted."

I started crying. My boyfriend hugged me and reassured me that I would be okay.

The doctor said, "We have to keep you until we can get you better."

I was upset because I was in a strange state and was thousands of miles from my home. I felt uncomfortable being in that hospital. I wanted my mama.

My boyfriend would come visit me in the daytime and then come spend the nights with me too. I was so drugged up with pain medicines that I barely remembered people coming to visit me, my memory was quite fuzzy.

I was in the hospital for a lot longer than I expected to be. I was there for about two weeks. I was deathly ill, and the doctors thought I might die. My family was scared that that crisis was going to be the one to end my life.

My mother was in California, stressed out. She called me every day to make sure I was okay. She tried to convince me to fly home with my son after they released me from the hospital. I had never flown before, due to being afraid of heights. I was going to fly when I was ready to, not when people tried to force me to. My uncle in Texas called me and also tried to convince me to fly, and I told him no. A few of my close family and friends also tried to do so, and I gave them the same answer. I was going to go home the same way I'd gotten to Mississippi, and that was to drive back with my boyfriend and our son Jayce.

When I got out of the hospital two weeks later, we ended up leaving my boyfriend's mother's house two days later. It had been a long drive to Mississippi, but the trip seemed a lot quicker on our way back to California. I was happy when we made it back to our place. My place looked different when I got home, because we had been gone for a lot longer than we'd expected to be. A trip that was supposed to be a week had turned into a three-week trip. I had lost quite a bit of weight while in the hospital. I am glad God blessed me to get home safe and sound. I thought I was going to die, but once again, God had saved me and spared my life.

CHAPTER 15

Another Pregnancy Loss

When I was thirty-six years old, I suffered a miscarriage with my fifth baby. I was almost three months pregnant. I was not even aware I was pregnant. We had just moved back to California from Texas one year prior to my becoming pregnant. I was not excited to be pregnant, because my boyfriend and I were having a lot of personal issues and were not in a good place in our relationship. The baby was a blessing from God. However, I knew a baby would not be a good thing at that moment because our relationship was so rocky. I knew the baby would not fix our broken relationship but would just add more responsibility to my already chaotic life. I more than likely was going to be a single mom because we were in the process of separating.

I went to a hair shop to get my hair permed and styled. The beautician said, "Girl, you do not look good."

I ran into the restroom and threw up. I did not want her to know I was pregnant. But I was sweating and pale. I shared with her that I was expecting, because she kept asking me personal questions. I had not ever met her. It was my first time going to her shop.

Once I told her I was pregnant, she calmed down and stopped asking me questions. She said, "Congratulations!"

I smiled as if I were happy, but I was sad inside. I felt guilty as a mom because I already had a son, and I loved being his mom. I felt incapable of being someone else's mom at that moment. I knew that was selfish, but that was how I felt.

The day I found out, I went to the emergency room alone. I never went unaccompanied; however, I did that particular day. I was in a mild crisis, so I had to go to the hospital. I dreaded going there because I knew I would have to get an IV and that they were going to have a hard time putting it in. Regardless of my feelings, I had no choice. My leg was throbbing, and I was in a lot of pain.

Once I got to the hospital, I went to the front desk. The nurse asked me, "Ma'am, how can I assist you?"

I said, "Ma'am, I have sickle cell anemia, and I'm currently in a crisis."

She said, "Where is your pain, ma'am?"

"My left leg is hurting really bad."

"Okay, please follow me; we need to check your temperature and your blood pressure."

They took me to the back and put me in a room. The doctor came into my room a few minutes later. She introduced herself to me. She said, "What do they usually do for you?"

I looked at her. *Why do all doctors always ask me, "So what should we do to help you?" I'm no doctor.* I hated when a doctor asked me those kinds of questions. But I was used to it. I said, "Well, they usually give me morphine, IV fluids, and an oxygen mask."

She said, "Sounds good." She had a nurse come attempt to give me an IV.

The nurse stuck me five times and had no success.

The doctor walked back into my room and said, "We are having a hard time starting an IV for you. We are going to have to do something different."

She left for about ten minutes, and then she came back. I was used to getting an IV in my arm, but the doctor said, "I might have to put an IV in your neck."

I sat up straight in my hospital bed. "My neck?"

She looked at me and said, "Oh, you've never had an IV in your neck?"

I shook my head like a little child who had done something wrong and was not telling her mom the truth. I was scared.

She said, "It's no different from putting an IV in your arm."

I looked at her as if she were crazy. It was quite different to me because I thought an IV belonged in the arm, not the neck. I was afraid, but I had to get the IV.

I'd never had a doctor give me a shot; usually, he or she had the nurse do it, but the doctor said, "I will put your IV in myself. I usually do not do shots, but I will administer it for you. Please give me a few minutes to go get the stuff so I can prepare to put your IV in."

She left for a few minutes. My anxiety had basically subsided because I knew I had to get the IV in my neck to feel better. The doctor came back into the room with all the supplies for the IV she was going to put in my neck. I tried to be patient and pretend I was okay, but I was nervous. I felt like the lion from *The Wizard of Oz*; I wanted to run and jump out the nearest window, as he did in the movie. But I just lay there and anticipated how much it would hurt as well as how uncomfortable I would feel.

She was genuinely nice and patient with me. She prepped me and explained everything she was going to do to me before she did it. She made me comfortable in an awkward moment. She was good, because I did not really feel the needle when she put it in. However, I did feel the cold saline fluid traveling down my neck. It was not painful at all; however, the thought of an IV in my neck was unnerving because I had never experienced that. I had an uncle, now deceased, who also had sickle cell anemia and was a difficult stick, and they had a challenging time putting IVs in him as well. They would put IVs anywhere they could possibly put them in his body. He told me they would put IVs in his foot, his leg, or even his neck.

I already felt uneasy with having an IV in my arm, let alone anywhere else in my body. Plus, I hated needles with a passion.

She was done quickly. She said, "I need to run some much-needed tests on you." She had someone from the lab come draw my blood. The doctor and nurse left, so I attempted to get a little rest.

I slept for about two hours, and then the doctor returned. She said, "Your tests all turned out negative except one." I looked at her crazily. She said, "You tested positive for one test."

I sat straight up because I was in immediate panic mode.

She saw my facial expression and smiled. She said, "Please just calm down. I have some good news. This test is positive because you are going to have a baby."

I looked at her as if to say, "Are you kidding me?"

She smiled. She said, "Are you okay?"

I managed a weak smile and said, "Oh, I'm just so surprised." I had been unaware that I was pregnant. I did not feel sick, weak, or otherwise pregnant.

She said, "You are almost three months pregnant. Please go see your ob-gyn as soon as possible. I will send the nurse in here in a few minutes to take that IV out for you."

After the nurse left the room, I just sat there trying to take in all the information. I thought, *Wow, I am not ready to be a mama to another child.* I took it all in for a few more minutes, and then I left.

When I got in my car, I cried. I was emotional at that moment. I was mad, sad, glad, and angry all at one time. After I wiped my tears away, I exhaled and decided to call my mother first because she always can comfort me when I am not in a good place. I called her. She answered. I said, "Hey, Mom, how are you doing?"

She said, "I'm hanging in there. How are you?"

I said, "I'm okay. I have something I would like to share with you." I took a deep breath. "I just went to the emergency room."

"Are you okay?"

"Mama, I'm in a mild crisis, but I'm okay. They ran some tests, and all the results were negative except one."

She said, "What? Are you okay?"

I said, "Mama, I'm okay. I just found out that I'm almost three months pregnant."

She said, "Oh, that's good. I'm glad you are not sick and don't have something deadly wrong with you. Congratulations."

I said, "Thank you, Mom. I will tell my siblings that I am pregnant when I get bigger." I hung up the phone.

When I got home, my boyfriend and my son were watching TV. I walked into the apartment and laid my purse down. My son ran over and hugged me. He was five years old. I picked him up and kissed him. I said, "Mommy is going to have a baby."

My son laughed. He started clapping. He was happy.

My boyfriend walked over to me. He said, "Oh, you are pregnant?"

I looked at him and said in a sarcastic way, "Yes, I'm pregnant."

He said, "How do you feel about being pregnant?"

I looked at him as if he were crazy. I said, "I feel this baby is a blessing from God. God does not make mistakes."

He smiled. He seemed happy. I was glad he was happy, because I was confused. My emotions were all over the place.

I did not want my place of employment to know I was pregnant. I was working with two of my good friends, and we loved working together. However, they were both going to be leaving in a few days. A friend I had known for more than thirteen years worked in the same class I did. Her family was well known for having psychic abilities. Her mother was good at reading people.

I believe in God—let me put that out first and foremost. However, I do believe God gives some people the ability to see things.

My friend asked if she could read me. I gave her my hand. I had not shared with her that I was pregnant, because I did not want anyone to know. She said, "Hey, are you pregnant?"

I smiled. I denied it at first. I said, "No, I'm not pregnant."

She looked at me and said, "I do not believe you. Are you pregnant?"

After about five minutes of her badgering me, I said, "Okay, yes, I'm pregnant."

She said, "You always have boys, but this one will most likely be a girl." I looked at her. She kept reading me. Then her facial expression changed instantly. She said, "Wow."

I said, "What is wrong?"

She looked sad. I knew she did not want to share what she saw with me. She said, "I should have let my younger sister read you." Her younger sister was good at reading people too. "I'm done." She looked at me, and I looked at her. We did not discuss my reading any more that day.

I knew I was headed for trouble. I spoke with her years later, and she explained to me what she had seen. She said, "I saw that you were pregnant with a girl, but she was going to pass because you were going to miscarry. I just did not want to tell you. I knew you always wanted another child." She was not aware that my boyfriend and I were on the verge of separation while I was pregnant. She felt bad for me, but I explained to her that I knew it was not meant for me to have that baby.

My two friends quit, and the school hired two new staff members I did not know. I was a little uncomfortable because the two new women were complete strangers I had not ever worked with and didn't know. I'm a people person, but it takes a while for me to warm up to new people. I must get to know people before I can develop a friendship with them.

When they first started working with me, they used to always whisper between themselves. I told them, "When you whisper, you are being impolite." They kept whispering for a few weeks, and then they finally stopped. I wanted to tell them I was pregnant, but the way they were whispering and carrying on, I decided not to say anything to either one of them.

We had little cots the kids slept on. They weighed about ten pounds or more. I knew I should not have been picking up those cots, but I did it because I did not want them to think I was lazy or just not willing to be a team player. I picked up three cots at a time, which made the weight thirty pounds versus ten. I picked up beds every day.

I decided to tell my siblings I was pregnant. My little sister and my little brother were excited when I told them. My sister asked me if she and my brother could name the baby. I said, "Sure, I do not have any ideas for names at the moment." My other siblings were excited as well but not as excited as my youngest two siblings.

But that joy was short-lived. I ended up miscarrying that baby three weeks later.

I was at a shopping center near my house by myself. I was browsing in the store, when I started getting massive cramps. The cramps were worse than labor pains. I had some items in my basket, but I was in so much pain that I just left the whole basket and left the store. I called my boyfriend and said, "I think you are going to have to take me to the emergency room, because I'm having massive cramps." He asked me where I was, and I said, "I'm at the shopping center up the street. I will be home in five minutes." I hung up.

It took me a few minutes longer than five minutes due to the pain I was in. I parked the car and ran to my front door. My boyfriend answered the door. I felt something in my pants. I immediately walked to my room and went and used the bathroom. I was sitting on the toilet, when I felt something slither and then pass and drop into the toilet. I stood up and looked in the toilet, and I saw a blood clot the size of a golf ball. It scared me.

I yelled for my boyfriend, and he ran into our room and into the bathroom. I said, "Look—that is a blood clot. I need to get to the hospital right now."

He said, "Okay, pull your pants up, and let's go." I pulled my pants up, and we left.

I called my mom. I said, "Mom, I think I'm having a miscarriage."

My mama said, "How do you know?"

I started crying. I said, "I was at a shopping center, and I started having massive cramps, worse than labor pains. I left and went home. When I got home, I was in the bathroom, and I felt something slither out of my body. I stood up, and it was a blood clot as big as a golf ball."

She gasped. She said, "Did you keep it so you can show the doctor when you get to the emergency room?"

I said, "No, Mama."

She said, "You have to always do that so they can figure out what is wrong with you."

I started crying because the pains were getting worse by the second. We pulled up to my mom's house. My mother was standing at the door, in her doorway. I told my son to get out. My mama said, "I love you." I was hollering and screaming because I was in severe pain. My mama told my boyfriend, "Hurry. Please just get her to the hospital."

He backed the car up and sped all the way to the hospital. Even though the hospital was only ten minutes away, it seemed it took us an hour to get there, and he was driving pretty fast. I thought we were going to get a speeding ticket. If the police pulled us over, I was ready with my tears and my pain.

When we arrived at the hospital, my boyfriend explained to the nurse sitting at the window that I was having a miscarriage. Her eyes got as big as golf balls. She said, "I need her name, please. I must ask you a few questions before we are able to treat her."

He said, "Okay, but can you please hurry? Because she is in a lot of pain."

I was screaming and hollering loudly. She looked at me as if I were crazy. She said, "Okay, let me get someone to get her a wheelchair." She got on the PA system and called for a nurse and a wheelchair. A nurse came with a wheelchair and assisted me into it and wheeled me to the back. They put me in a room. I was crying because I was hurting so much.

An Asian doctor walked in. He introduced himself to me and my boyfriend. He asked me why I was there. I just looked at him. I was in too much pain to answer him. My boyfriend said, "She passed a blood clot as big as a golf ball in the toilet when she used the bathroom. Before she passed the blood clot, she was at a shopping center, and she started cramping bad."

He looked at my boyfriend and then back at me. He said, "How many kids does she have?"

My boyfriend looked at the doctor strangely. He said, "We have one son."

The doctor said, "How old is her son?"

My boyfriend said, "Our son is five years old."

He said, "She is still young, so she will be able to have more babies. We will have to let her pass this baby." He kept looking at me and then at my boyfriend. "Is this her first time losing a baby?"

My boyfriend said, "No. We lost two sons prior to our son we have now. She also lost a baby a few years ago, but we were not even aware she was pregnant."

He said, "Okay, well, there is nothing I can do for her; she will have to just lose the baby." I cried even more. The doctor looked at me. He said, "I will be back in a little while to check on her." He left.

I was hollering. My boyfriend was just looking at me. He looked helpless. He could not do anything to help me. I suddenly felt the urge to use the bathroom. I told my boyfriend I had to pee. He helped me get up, and he tied my hospital gown in the back. He walked me to the restroom. I went inside the bathroom by myself, and he stood outside and waited for me.

I sat on the toilet, and as soon as I opened my legs to use the bathroom, I felt a huge ball-like substance drop out of me. I was afraid to stand up and look, but I knew I had to see what had just fallen into the toilet. I stood up slowly. I looked in the toilet. I saw a fetus, my baby, lying in the toilet. I screamed.

My boyfriend said, "Babe, is everything okay?"

I unlocked the door and let him in. I said, "Look in the toilet."

He walked over slowly and peeked in the toilet. He looked sad. He shook his head and said, "Wow." All the pain suddenly vanished into thin air.

My boyfriend went and got the nurse. The nurse went and got the doctor. The doctor said, "Okay, you passed the baby."

I said, "Do you need to see it?"

He looked at me as if I had cussed him out or disrespected him in the wrong way. He said, "No, I do not want to see it. It is a dead fetus." He did not even care that I had just lost my baby. He told the nurse to take care of the fetus, and he walked away. He was a rude man.

I went into my room and got dressed, and we left the hospital. I did not speak at all during the ride to pick my son up. We picked my son up, and we all went home. I lay in my bed all weekend.

My boyfriend and I separated several months later. I was now a single mom once again.

CHAPTER 16

Grief and a Trip to San Diego

When I was thirty-eight years old, I suffered another horrific crisis. My brother was murdered, and my family and I were grieving. The loss of my brother almost killed me. My brother and I always had been close because I'd helped my mother raise my little brother along with my siblings. He was my only little brother and my mother's only living son. Burying my brother was probably the hardest thing I ever had to do in my life. It was hard to go to the funeral home, pick out a casket, select flowers, and choose the right music for his funeral.

I have always written poetry, and I wrote a personal poem for my brother that I read at his funeral. Reading that poem was hard for me, but my brother gave me strength and the ability to get up in front of a lot of people and read it. My brother spoke to me spiritually and told me to pretend that no one else was in the room and to read it just to him. My seven-year-old son went with me when I went up to the podium. He was my support system.

We had my brother's funeral a week after he got murdered. His death was life-changing for me and my family. My mother had five girls and two boys. However, both her sons were now deceased. Losing my sons Keon and Kenneth did not affect me as much as losing my little brother did, because he had been my first baby in a way. I was and still am heartbroken. I will never get over his death.

My son had a candy fundraiser, so I decided to take the fundraiser paper to my job. I intended to sell some candy but not as much as I ended up selling. I think my coworkers felt sorry for me and for my family's loss, so they went all out and purchased a lot from me and my son. I sold $674 worth of candy in two days.

My son sold the most candy in his entire school. He received all the prizes and the grand prize as well. The grand prize was a seven-day, six-night vacation stay in San Diego, at a golf resort. Although my son won the trip because he sold the most candy in the school, I was not going to let him go, due to his horrible grades. I decided to take my youngest niece instead, who was a straight-A student. I felt she deserved the trip a lot more than my son did. I felt bad that my son was going to miss out on the trip, but he had to face a consequence for his bad grades in school. People in my life felt I was wrong, but I had to teach my son a lesson. I felt bad.

The day we were leaving, my son packed his suitcase and put it in our car.

I said, "Jayce, why did you pack your suitcase? I already packed your bag for Nana's house."

He started crying. He said, "Mom, I will bring my grades up. I promise."

My eyes started watering. I was about to cry. We drove to my mom's house, which was about five minutes from my apartment. My niece was going to spend the night at my house so we could get up at four o'clock and leave early in the morning. When I got to my mom's house, my niece was ready. She hugged her mom and her nana and kissed them both and said goodbye. I hugged my son and kissed him and said goodbye. He cried.

I walked outside, and I cried on the drive home to my apartment. My niece hugged me and said, "Jayce will be fine."

I woke up at three o'clock in the morning, took a shower, and got dressed. I woke my niece up so she could shower and get dressed. We left at four o'clock. San Diego was eight hours from where we lived.

I had never driven that far by myself without another driver. My niece was only eleven years old and was not able to drive yet. It was just the two of us. I was a little sleepy, so we stopped by a gas station, and I got some coffee because it always made me wake up. As I was driving, I realized I'd better play my mood music. I loved hip-hop, so I put on a rap CD. My niece noticed I had not drunk my coffee yet. I looked at her and said, "When I hear hip-hop music, I immediately wake up." I drank my coffee.

I was rolling, not realizing I was going over the speed limit, because we got there too quick. An eight-hour drive took me six hours. We stopped for gas a few times. When we got to the golf resort, we were both tired.

We stopped by a restaurant, picked up some food, and then went to our room and ate. After we ate, we both decided to take a nap. We took a two-hour nap, and then we went to the pool at the golf resort. My niece got in because she knew how to swim. I just sat in a chair, watching her. I met a nice older white couple who were at the pool with us. We talked while my niece swam. I was glad they were there, because I did not swim, as I did not know how. We stayed there for a few hours, and then we went and got some food at a local restaurant. We took our food back to our room. We watched TV until we got so sleepy our eyes started closing. We went to sleep.

The next morning, we decided to go to the San Diego Zoo. It is huge, and it takes three days to see the entire zoo. We got there at eleven o'clock and stayed until four. The zoo was humongous and exceptionally beautiful; it is one of the largest zoos in the world. We walked a lot. The zoo was nice but tiring.

After we left the zoo, we were so exhausted we went back to our hotel and ate and then took a nap. After we woke up from our nap, we went to the pool. My niece decided to get into the pool and then into the Jacuzzi. She really liked getting in the Jacuzzi. She said the water was warm. She said, "Get in, Tee-Tee."

I smiled at her. I said, "No, Auntie cannot get in, because I might get sick."

She said, "Oh, okay, but the water feels good."

The next day, we decided to go to Sea World. Sea World was beautiful. The animals were amazing. It was an undertaking; we walked for hours. Once again, we were tired after all the walking we did that day. We left Sea World, went and got food, and then went back to our hotel. We rested for a while and then went to the pool. We stayed at the pool for hours. My niece was having a great time. We went to our hotel room when the sun went down.

The next day, we slept in and did not get out until about three o'clock. We attempted to go to a safari park where you can ride on a bus and go out to see and touch the animals. However, when we got there, we'd missed the last bus ride. We were both disappointed. We both had wanted to see all the beautiful animals up close. We stayed at the safari park for an hour and walked around. Then we went into the gift shop and bought some souvenirs for our family members.

The safari park was on a tall, steep hill, and I was a little nervous. My niece was extremely anxious. She said, "Tee-Tee, I do not like these hills. I am scared."

I told her, "Do not worry; I will protect you."

She was relieved when we finally made it back to the freeway. I was scared as hell, but I had to remain calm for my niece's sake. We left the safari park, went and ate, and then went back to our hotel. We relaxed for a little while, and then my niece wanted to go swimming. We went to the pool for a few hours. My niece swam until she was tired and sleepy. We watched TV and then went to bed.

The next day, we were still tired, so we ate breakfast at a local restaurant and then lay down and watched TV. A few hours later, we went to the pool. We stayed there for a few hours. We went out and got our dinner and brought it back to the hotel. We watched TV and then went to bed.

We had four more days until we were to go home, but we had seen all we wanted to see. I asked my niece if she wanted to stay for four more days. She smiled and said, "It's up to you, Tee-Tee."

I said, "When we wake up tomorrow, I will make my decision."

The next day, we got up and went and ate breakfast. I decided we would leave early in the morning so we could beat the traffic. My niece was ready to go home as well. Since it was our last day in San Diego, my niece wanted to go to the pool one last time.

It was hot outside. My niece was in the Jacuzzi, relaxing and having fun. I knew I should not get into the Jacuzzi, but I got in against my better judgment. I second-guessed myself, and I should not have. I should have followed my first instinct.

My niece looked at me and said, "Maybe you should not get in."

I looked at her and smiled. "I will only get in for a few minutes."

It was so hot outside that I never thought I would get sick. Boy, was I wrong.

I stayed in the Jacuzzi for about fifteen minutes, and then I got out. I lay on one of the pool lounge chairs and watched my niece splash around in the Jacuzzi. We stayed there for a few hours. Then we went back to our hotel room.

We packed up all our stuff. We went to the hotel restaurant and ordered some food to go. We went back to our room, ate, and watched television. After we watched television, we went to sleep.

I woke up at four o'clock and took a shower. Once I was done, I woke my niece up, she took a shower, and then we took our bags to the car. We checked out and then got on the road. We got home quicker than we'd gotten to San Diego. I dropped my niece off at home, and I picked my son up. I went home and unpacked my stuff and my son's stuff. It was late, so I fed my son, and he went to bed.

I woke up early the next day because I had a meeting to go to. I got up, took a shower, and got dressed. I woke my son up, he took a bath, and we both ate breakfast. I dropped him off at my mother's house while I went to the meeting. I had lunch with my friend Sheila, and then I went to pick up my son. We went home and watched some movies, and then we ate our dinner. We both went to sleep after we ate.

I awoke with chest pain, lower back pain, and leg pain. I looked over at the clock. It was four o'clock. I knew it was too early to wake my mother up. I just lay in my bed. I got up and took some pain medicine. I must have fallen asleep for a few hours, because when I woke up, it was eight o'clock.

I got dressed. I woke my son up and got him dressed. I was in extreme pain. I drove to my mother's house. I called her on the phone on my way to her house. I told her I was in a crisis.

When I got there, she said, "I'll call an ambulance."

I shook my head. I said, "Mama, I'll call one of my friends."

I called a friend, and she came right away. She took me to the hospital. I was in such a bad crisis they admitted me as soon as I got there. My friend stayed with me until they put me in my own room. I got morphine, IV fluids, and oxygen. They also gave me a blood transfusion. I called to let my mother know what was happening.

She said, "Klee, do not worry; I will take care of Jayce." I was a single mom once again.

Jayce was at my mother's house for three weeks while I was stuck in the hospital. My son's father called me more than a hundred times, but I did not feel well enough to talk to him. I did not feel like talking to anyone except my mother and siblings. I had hundreds of missed calls and text messages. I had my phone on vibrate the whole time I was in the hospital.

I lost fifty pounds in three weeks due to not having an appetite when in a crisis. I do not like food at all when I am sick. My mom, my son, my little sister, and one of my older sisters came to visit me. I remember them coming to see me, but my memory of that hospital stay is fuzzy. I remember when I first got to the hospital. I talked to my mother the first day I was there, but for the next two days, I was drugged up. My mama kept calling, and when I did not answer for those two days, she showed up at the hospital.

I was asleep, but I could hear my mama's voice. She said, "It's Mama."

I barely could open my eyes. I heard my son. He said, "Mama, are you okay?"

I opened my eyes. I smiled when I saw my son. I was so happy to see him. He climbed into my hospital bed and lay right next to me. He gave me the hope I needed to fight. I knew I had a purpose, and he was right next to me. He lay with me the whole time they were visiting me in the hospital. I was sad when they left. My son cried too. He helped me to perk up a little.

When I was released from the hospital, I had to go stay with my mother, sister, and niece, and of course, my son was there too. I stayed with my mother for about two weeks. I stayed there because I did not want to be home alone with my son. My mother had a couch bed, and my son and I slept on it. My mother took care of my son while I recuperated. My niece and my son were happy to see me. They would not let me out of their sight. They followed me everywhere I went. I went to the bathroom, and they waited for me outside the bathroom. They lay with me in the bed all day and made sure I was okay. They made sure I ate. We watched a lot of movies. I think my being gone for so long in the hospital traumatized them.

I was homesick after two weeks and decided to go home. My mother said, "You might need to stay a week longer."

I went home two weeks later. I was not fully well, but I was homesick. There is no place like home. I needed to be in my own bed. I was happy to be home. My mama called to check on me all day long every day.

I am glad I followed my first instinct and left San Diego earlier than I was supposed to. Only God knows what would have happened had I stayed the few extra days. It would have been a disaster.

CHAPTER 17

Napa

When I was about to turn forty years old, I had another major crisis. I got sick and had to be hospitalized. My mama had to watch my son for a week. I was at home with my son when I got sick. I had just put him in bed. I stayed up for a little while, watching television. I decided to go to bed. I lay down and fell asleep for a little while. I awoke with leg pains. I managed to get up and go get some pain medicine. It was not too late, so I decided to call my mother. I told her I was in a crisis.

My mother said, "Bring Jayce over here."

I was in pain, but I managed enough strength to wake my son up, get him dressed, and get him into the car. I drove to my mother's house. It was late.

My mother said, "You might need to go in an ambulance."

I said, "Mama, I'm not in too much pain." I decided to drive myself.

When I got to the hospital, I was admitted. I stayed in the hospital for a week. It was hard because I missed my son. I hated to be away from him.

I told my best friend I wanted to go to Napa Valley for my birthday. She said, "I've been there, and it's a cool place to go." I was happy because I had never been to Napa before. I had always wanted to go there, but I was not a drinker, so I did not see the purpose in going at first. But I'd heard it was beautiful. I had been wanting to go for years. This was a special occasion because I was going to be forty years old. That was a milestone birthday. I'd made it, when people had told me I would not make it. Man does not hold my future; God does. I can do all things through Christ, who strengthens me. That is a biblical verse I love and try to live by daily. There is nothing I cannot accomplish.

I drove from Sacramento to Fairfield, which was a forty-five-minute drive. I met my friend, and we went to her mom's house. We talked to her mom for a little while, and then we left. My friend drove because she knew how to get there since she had been there before.

We ate at a restaurant when we first got there. The food was expensive but not good at all. When we arrived in Napa, it was beautiful. The scenery was gorgeous. We parked the car and walked around to different vineyards. I saw Sutter Home. When I had had a drink back in the day on special occasions, I would drink a tiny glass of Sutter Home. We walked into the Sutter Home winery. I was blown away because they had nonalcoholic wine. I had not known they had nonalcoholic wine, and it was good. I was looking around at the different types of nonalcoholic wines, when I heard a familiar voice.

I thought I was dreaming, but I was not. I saw my best friend from childhood. She recognized me. We walked up to each other and hugged. We had not seen each other in more than twenty years. She looked the exact same, just a little older. We exchanged numbers and talked for about thirty minutes, and then my friend and I left. *Wow, a blast from my past.* I will always love her because she was there for me a lot when we were young. We were there for each other. We had a purpose to be friends when we were younger, and we were inseparable back then. I never imagined her not being in my life. I lost contact with a lot of friends who were a huge part of who I am.

CHAPTER 18

Wedding Bells

My boyfriend and I have been through a lot over the years. We have had our share of both good and bad days. I know no one has the perfect relationship, and if people say they do, they are not being honest. There is no perfect man but God. My boyfriend and I have been on a merry-go-round ride that I kept getting on and off.

We ended up breaking up in 2010 for three years. After we broke up, he moved. I was happy because he was out of sight and out of mind. I was happy he was gone. It was much easier because I did not have to see him.

However, his absence took a toll on our son. Jayce was distraught. He missed his daddy and would ask about him daily. I made sure my son still communicated with his daddy often. It was hard on me too. I used to cry myself to sleep at night after my son went to bed. I prayed a lot. I even prayed a sincere prayer that God would help my son's father and change him for the better. I said, "I would love to be back with him, but if we are not meant for each other, change him for another woman. Let the next woman he is with be a good woman and a great woman to my son. I just want him to be better, with me or without me." I prayed that prayer. God answered my prayer four years later.

Let's fast-forward to three years later. My son's father started calling me. At first, I was not happy to speak with him. I told him that my son was capable and old enough to answer the phone and speak with him. They talked all the time. He used to ask to talk to me.

God finally changed him. God answered my prayers. He moved back to Sacramento. He moved in with his brother and my sister. I took my son over to see him at their house when he first came back to town. He changed his life. He enrolled in school, started working with his brother, and changed overall. We had been together for ten years prior to breaking up.

He soon had been back in Sacramento for about a year, and we were coparenting. We were also trying to rekindle our relationship to see if we could possibly make it. In the beginning, we argued and did not get along. We decided maybe we were not meant to be. We continued to talk on the phone and see each other all the time, but I felt we were not really on the same page. I called him and said, "I love you, and I always will love you, but I cannot continue to do this back-and-forth thing. I am just going to move on."

He said, "I understand where you are coming from. You've got to do what you've got to do." I hung up.

We continued to hang out. Three weeks later, I was driving home from the store with my son, and he called me and said, "Hey, I think I want to marry you."

I laughed. I thought he was joking. I almost hit the car in front of me.

He said, "Why are you laughing at me?"

I continued to laugh. We hung up.

A week later, he said, "I need to go talk to your mama."

I looked at him and said, "Why do you need to go talk to my mom?"

He drove us to my mama's house. He had me go into my sister's room and close the door. He came and knocked on the office door fifteen minutes later, and we left. I thought the whole thing was strange.

The next day was Sunday, and my son was scheduled to be baptized that morning. I invited my sisters and my niece because I wanted them to see my son get baptized.

I was sitting in the back of the church, but after my son got baptized, they asked me to sit in the front, on the front pew. I thought that was odd. I knew something was happening. I went and sat up there. My son came and sat next to me. The next thing I knew, my son's father was up front, giving a testimony. He spoke about how I was a good woman and always had been there, no matter what he put me through. It was so touching that I cried. But what he did next made me cry even more. He walked toward me, and he got down on bended knee and proposed to me. I was so emotional that I was speechless. He said, "Will you marry me?"

I was unable to speak. All I could hear was my best friend's mom saying, "Say yes."

I nodded. I kept crying. I was overjoyed.

We got married four months later at the church where he proposed to me. We all started going to that church again. I had gone there in the past. We became members, and my husband is now a minister of the church. I am a youth director, and my son is an usher as well as a junior deacon.

I never wanted to be married. I was always afraid to do so. We were supposed to get married two years before my brother got murdered, but I called the wedding off because my husband was not ready yet.

However, God is good all the time, and all the time God is good. He answered my prayer. He changed my husband, who has been doing great. We have been married for six years now. Our marriage is good. But marriage takes a lot of work. Communication and negotiation are the keys to making a marriage work. Being married to me can be difficult because I speak my mind. The fact that I have sickle cell anemia can be hard for my husband to deal with too. But he is good with me, and he deals with my disease.

CHAPTER 19

Overwhelmed

A month before I turned forty-two years old, I felt as if I had a dark cloud over me. All the things I went through would be enough to make anyone say, "Wow." Some probably would have given up. But I was born a fighter. I will fight to the end.

I was at work, and I started having bad stomach pains. A coworker said, "You do not look good. What is wrong?"

I said, "I'm okay." But my face was saying something else.

I tried to sit down; I was hurting. I tried to stand up; I was hurting. The pain was constant and excruciating. I was hurting so much I decided to go home early. I called my husband so he could go get our son from school.

My husband went and got us some food from one of my favorite restaurants. I was home, still in pain. He said, "Eat, babe. You might feel better."

I ate one egg roll, and I immediately got sick. My husband went and got me some Pepto-Bismol from the store. When he got back from the store, he gave me some. I drank it, and I immediately threw up. I was on the floor in pain.

He said, "Babe, I'm taking you to the emergency room."

He took me to the hospital. They saw how much pain I was in, and they took me right to a room. They gave me a test in an MRI-type machine. They put me in the machine and told me the process could take a minute to forty-five minutes. They said it might be quick, because for some people, it gave instant results. I got in the machine and was in there for one minute, and it gave me an instant result. The technician took me out of the machine and rolled me back to my room. My husband and son were sitting there, waiting on me.

I had been back in my room for about five minutes, when a doctor walked in. He introduced himself. He asked me how I was feeling.

I looked at him. How did he think I was feeling? *If I were feeling good, then I would be at home, not wasting my time at the hospital.* I said, "I'm still in a lot of pain."

He said, "Well, it looks like you have a gallstone, and it is in a pretty bad place in your body. We will need to perform gallbladder surgery to remove the stone. We will have to admit you into the hospital and do the surgery immediately." My eyes got big. He said, "Calm down; we will perform the surgery early in the morning."

I was a little relieved.

He said, "Would you like some pain medicine?"

I said, "Yes, I would like some medicine, please."

The nurse walked in and gave me some pain medicine. The nurse said the doctor who would perform my surgery would be coming in to speak with me.

I was dozing off, when a petite doctor about four feet tall or maybe even shorter walked into my room. I thought I was dreaming or drugged up. She introduced herself to me and to my husband and my son. She got a stool and stood by my bed. She said, "I will be doing your surgery tomorrow morning." She showed me an x-ray of a stone near my vital organs. She said, "Usually people have lots of stones, but you only have one. When there is only one, we can usually leave it alone, but the one you have is in a dangerous spot." They had to take it out, or it could affect some of my vital organs. She wished me luck and said, "I will see you first thing in the morning."

When she left, I started crying. My husband hugged me and reassured me that I was going to be okay. My son hugged me and kissed me because they were leaving. My husband hugged and kissed me again. He said, "Babe, I will be here in the morning for your surgery."

When my husband and my son left, I cried again. I hated having surgery. I hated the unnatural sleep. I have had surgeries during which I had out-of-body experiences. I hate telling people about my out-of-body experiences because people can be so closed-minded.

I prayed and asked God to protect me and keep me safe. I could not wait for the surgery to be over. I had a hard time sleeping. I did not sleep at all. I was up worrying. I looked up, and the sun was rising.

The nurse came and prepped me for my surgery. She said, "How are you feeling, dear?" I looked at her, and she knew something was wrong. She said, "Oh, please do not worry; it is a simple and quick surgery. I just had the surgery a few weeks ago." She made me feel comfortable. My anxiety was a lot less. She prayed with me, and that brought me a lot of peace.

My husband walked into my room. I was glad to see him. He said, "Babe, I will be in the waiting room when you are done."

She rolled me into the surgery room. I do not remember anything but counting backward, and then I was sleeping. I woke up in the recovery room.

The nurse went and got my husband. I smiled when he walked into the room. I was in a lot of pain. The nurse gave me some pain medicine. I had to stay overnight because they felt they needed to watch me due to my having sickle cell anemia. I got out the following day. I was in a lot of pain.

The nurse lied; it took me almost six weeks to fully recover. It was hard after my surgery to get around at home. It was hard to go to the bathroom, bathe, or even walk well, as I was in so much pain.

A few weeks later, my husband, my son, and I decided to go see a movie. We arrived at the movie theater and found our seats. My son said, "Mom, I do not feel well. I am going to the bathroom." He walked to the bathroom.

He was gone for about ten minutes; I got a little worried. I decided to go check on my son. He was only ten years old. I was just about to walk out of the movie theater, when I slipped. It felt as if I were falling in slow motion. I was unable to stop myself from falling. I fell. Once I was on the ground, I was unable to get up. I tried to get up, but I could not.

An older white couple walked by. They saw me trying to get up. The man walked up to me and tried to assist me. He said, "I'm an ex-cop, and if you cannot get up, your leg is definitely broken." I told his wife to go get my husband for me. She went and got him.

My husband came and attempted to pick me up, but the ex-cop said, "No, please do not move her, because her leg may be broken."

The manager walked up to us. He said, "Ma'am, what happened to you?"

I was in a lot of pain. I was barely able to talk. I said, "I was walking out of the theater, and I slipped."

He asked me to move over a little bit. There was a wet substance that looked like spit. He said, "Okay, I'm going to call 911 and have an ambulance come pick you up."

My son walked up to his dad. He looked at me. He said, "Mama, are you okay?"

I said, "Mama slipped and fell."

The ambulance arrived ten minutes later. Six EMT guys put me on a gurney. They put me in an ambulance. I was in pain. My husband and son followed the ambulance to the hospital.

Once we got to the hospital, they put me in a room, and my husband checked my son into the hospital too. We were in two different rooms, and my poor husband was going back and forth from my room to our son's room. They had to put an Ace bandage on my leg. They also put me in a walking cast.

I went to work a few weeks later. They put me on light duty. I was working in an office with some other coworkers helping them out. It was hard to get around on crutches, and I was still in pain from my gallbladder surgery. I started hurting in my rib area. I went to the doctor, and they diagnosed me with pneumonia. I was done. I was going through too much in my life. What else was going to happen to me? I just did not want to go into a crisis. I knew it was possible for me to do so because I was under so much stress. Stress can cause me to go into a crisis; plus, I had just had my gallbladder surgery, broken my ankle, and had pneumonia. I had just turned forty-two years old a few weeks ago, but I was miserable. It was already turning out bad. I just wanted that year to be over.

CHAPTER 20

Infection

The next year, I turned forty-three, and it was not a good year either. In the middle of the year, I had a bad crisis. I was at work, and I was not feeling well, but I made it through the day. It was hard, but I survived. When I got home, I lay down in my bed. My husband came home and noticed I was lying down in the bed. He asked me if I was okay. I said, "No, I'm not feeling well at all." He asked if I needed to go to the emergency room. I nodded.

He said, "Okay, let's go so we can get back home." We got in the car. He knew I was not feeling well, because I usually did not ever want to go to the hospital. I hated hospitals.

We drove to the hospital, and I was feeling weak and was sweating profusely. My husband kept looking at me. He said, "Babe, you really look bad. Please do not take that the wrong way." I smiled at him.

We dropped my son off at my mom's house and drove to the hospital. We went to the front desk, and they proceeded to check me in. The lady at the desk asked me, "What's going on with you, ma'am?"

I said, "I have sickle cell, diabetes, and high blood pressure. However, I feel weak, and I'm sweating to death."

"Okay," she said, "Come back so we can check your temperature and your blood pressure."

They checked my vitals and took me to a private room. Once I was in my room, the nurse started an IV on me. They ran a couple of tests on me.

The doctor came back a few hours later. He said, "You have an infection."

I sat up. "What kind of infection do I have?"

He said, "I'm not sure exactly where it is, but we will start giving you antibiotics to get rid of the infection."

They kept me for a few more hours, and then they sent me home. I went home and went to bed. The doctor gave me three days off work so I could rest. I needed the rest of the week off.

I had a hair appointment to get my hair braided that Saturday. I still was not feeling all that well, but I went and got my hair done. While I was at the hair shop and in the process of getting my hair braided, I started sweating a lot. The braider asked me if I was okay. I said, "Yes, but I am not really feeling well."

After she was done with my hair, I left and went home. When I got home, I was still sweating and not feeling well. I lay down in my bed. My husband noticed I was sleepy. He asked me how I was feeling. I told him I felt weak and was sleepy. He decided to take me to the hospital. We had just left the hospital only three days ago.

The nurse at the desk said, "How may I help you two?"

My husband said, "She just left three days ago, and she feels weak. She has an infection, sickle cell, diabetes, and high blood pressure. But they should have made her stay the other day."

I could tell the nurse was getting agitated. She said, "Okay, please follow me so we can check your blood pressure and check your temperature."

I had a 102-degree fever. They took me to the back and put me in my own room. I was in there for a few minutes, when a doctor walked in and introduced himself to me and my husband. He said, "We are going to run a few tests on you so we can see why you are weak and feeling so tired. In the meantime, we will give you morphine, IV fluids, and an oxygen mask to help with your breathing. Does that sound like a plan?"

I managed a smile. I said, "Yes, sounds like a great plan."

He left, and a nurse came in and started an IV. I hated IVs, but I had to get one to feel better.

The doctor came back a few hours later, and he had a peculiar look on his face. He said, "You have an infection. I think it's due to diabetes. You mentioned a cyst on your breast. You have an infection in your breast, and we are going to have to do immediate surgery." My heart dropped. He said, "We have to get the infection out because it is like poison in your body. We will do the surgery in the morning. But we must do a CAT scan immediately."

I had never had a CAT scan, so I was a little nervous.

I ended up being in the hospital for about three weeks. The surgery went well. However, for the next two months after my surgery, I had a long, deep hole in my breast, and I had to go to the emergency room once a week for a nurse to clean it out and repack it with clean cloths. It was painful. I hated to go to the emergency room and do that weekly, but I did not trust my husband to do it at home. I lost fifty pounds. Once again, I was unable to eat any food, because I was not feeling well.

I went back to work a month after my surgery. I had lost a lot of weight, and people made a lot of comments. They told me that I looked pale, and I still did not look well. It was hard to work, but I managed to perform my job.

A few weeks later, I started sweating profusely once more at work. My coworkers told me I did not look well. I went home early. I ended up getting sick again. I had to go back to the hospital again. The infection was getting better, but my body was still fighting it. I ended up having to stay home for two more weeks so I could fully recover.

Unfortunately, things ended up getting worse. I was readmitted into the hospital three weeks later. I ended up going into a major crisis. I had to get what is known as a PIC line. It's a catheter utilized for a prolonged period. It enters the body through the skin. They stuck a long plastic tool in my arm and left it in place. It was uncomfortable and made me feel uneasy. It can cause blood clots. They gave me Dilantin because they said it was ten times stronger than morphine. I do not like Dilantin at all. It made me hallucinate. Morphine did not do that to me. Both are pain medicines, but one is much worse to me. I have always preferred morphine.

The crisis caused me to have to get two blood transfusions. I was so drugged up, my husband said, I would take off my nightgown. I would complain about being hot. He said he brought my son to see me one day, and they had to leave because I refused to keep my gown on. I do not even remember that happening. My husband used to be upset with me. He would come up to the hospital to see me and would leave if my nightgown was off.

One night, I was completely upside down in my hospital bed, lying at the foot of the bed. I was yelling at the top of my lungs. "Somebody help me! I'm thirsty! I need some water! I'm thirsty!"

A black male doctor walked into my room. He said, "Young lady, how did you get down there? Let me help you." He assisted me in getting back to the right end of the bed. He fixed my gown. He went and got me some water.

The next morning, I was back at the foot of my bed. I had even pulled my IV out. They had to put a new IV in my arm. I had to get the two blood transfusions.

A male nurse came to give me the blood transfusions, but I refused to cooperate with him, so they had to call my husband. My husband and son came to the hospital the next day and forced me to get the blood transfusions. I was so sick that I was delusional. I know it was the Dilantin. Morphine did not cause me to act like that.

I had purchased tickets to go see my favorite singer in concert, and the concert was in a few weeks. I was contemplating if I was going to go, because I was still weak. I managed enough strength to make it to his concert. The concert was amazing. I stood up and danced and sang, even though I was not 100 percent well. I had been a fan since I was nineteen years old.

CHAPTER 21

A New Job and a New Purpose amid a Severe Crisis

When I turned forty-four years old, I had another major crisis. I was at home, and as usual, my chest started hurting. I knew it was a chest crisis, and I needed to go to the emergency room. When I was a little girl, my primary doctor always told me and my mother that when I got a chest crisis, I should get to the emergency room immediately. He always said that a chest crisis was nothing to play with. He was an awesome doctor. I was his patient from five years old until seventeen years old. We moved from San Francisco to Sacramento, and I established a new doctor. When I turned seventeen years old, my previous doctor died in a biking accident while he was on vacation overseas. I was sad when my mother told me the news. He was patient as well as nice to me. I liked him a lot.

I woke my husband up, and he said, "Okay, get dressed."

I was hurting so much that getting dressed was hard to do, but I did it. We had to wake our son up. We all got in the car, and my husband drove me to the hospital.

When we got there, it was crowded. I knew I was going to have to suffer for a while in the waiting room. But they took me to the back and set me in a chair in the hallway. We waited in the hallway for about two hours before they took me to my own room. My chest was really hurting. They gave me an EKG to make sure I was not having a heart attack. I was in so much pain. They started an IV and gave me Dilantin and oxygen. I was embarrassed because other patients and their families were staring at me as if I were a zoo animal or an alien. But I was in so much pain that I did not care who was looking at me.

My husband and my son were forced to wait in the waiting room due to the hospital's being overcrowded. They took turns coming to check on me every thirty minutes. I was drugged up, so although I remember them, the memory is vague for me. I remember an old lady hollering loudly. I must have been in the hallway for about four hours before they put me in a room.

A doctor came in and introduced himself to me, my husband, and my son. He said, "You are in a bad crisis. We will have to give you a blood transfusion. Your blood levels are low. We will have to admit you."

I started crying. I hated hospitals, and I especially hated to stay overnight in them. I was never able to sleep, because they would always poke and prod me every hour or two. How was I supposed to sleep?

My husband and son stayed until they put me in a room. They put me in the heart attack ward, where they put mainly elderly people. They claimed that was the only room available at the time. Once I got in the room, my husband and my son left. I was in the room all alone.

I was in the hospital for a week. He could not stay overnight with me because we had our son. He asked my sister to stay with me. She stayed with me for a couple of days. I was drugged up when my sister stayed with me. I was seeing things and hallucinating from the Dilantin. In school, I'd read a poem about a woman who went crazy and thought she lived in the yellow wallpaper. I told my sister I saw a lady go into the wallpaper at night. There was wallpaper in my room. My sister kept looking at me as if I were crazy.

Once again, I had to get another PIC line. I did not want it. However, they told my husband it would be beneficial for me because they could give me necessary shots through the PIC line. However, they continuously kept sticking me. They came in to stick me, and my husband happened to be there. He said, "Excuse me, but why are you about to stick her, when she has that PIC line in her arm?"

The nurse looked at him. She said, "We cannot draw blood from a PIC line."

He said, "Why did they even put a PIC line in her arm if they were still going to have to be sticking her all the time?"

The nurse just looked at him. She said, "You will have to ask her doctor." She did a blood test, and she left the room.

My husband said, "That is dumb." I thought it was dumb too.

I ended up going home. I had lost another fifty pounds in three weeks. I thought I looked good fifty pounds lighter. I looked healthier. I even felt healthier. It took me much longer to recover.

I went to work, even though I was still weak. My students were graduating from preschool and being promoted to kindergarten. I'd had some of my children for three years, some for two years, and some for one year. I felt I had to be there so I could tell them goodbye in person. Even though I was weak, I made it through their graduation ceremony. The children and parents were happy to see me. When I had been absent for three weeks, they had not been told anything about my whereabouts. I felt bad, because I had great relationships with the children and their families too. I was friends with some of the parents because we had been together for some years.

I resigned from the job I had been at for about twenty-four years, and I got promoted to a much better position, which I still currently hold: site supervisor and lead teacher. I decided I needed a change; plus, the new job is closer to my house.

I thought I was going to die from that crisis and felt I should just give up. But God said, "It's not your time to go."

As I said, my brother had been murdered in 2012, and I missed him so. I begged my brother to come meet me so I could die. I could not hear him physically, but his spirit spoke to me. He said, "You are a fighter. You've got to fight like you have never fought before. Your son needs you, and so does our mama." I always felt him with me when I was in the hospital, and I still do. He was always by my side. I know he was right. I decided to fight.

Prior to really trying to fight, I scared a lot of my family and friends. My husband was scared that this crisis was going to kill me. My mother and my siblings were all worried. I knew my son needed me the most.

I gave my husband my credit cards and told him where all my important documents were in our apartment. I wanted him to have all the things he would need in case I died at the hospital. He stayed strong, but I could see the fear in his eyes. He had to be tough for me, but I knew he was scared. I had a long conversation with him in which we discussed our life insurance policies and other necessary information in case something did happen to me.

I made it, though. God kept me. I'm glad he allowed me to still be here for my son, my husband, and my family and friends. I knew I had a special purpose at that moment. I had a story to tell, and I had to tell it to inspire other people who have sickle cell anemia.

CHAPTER 22

A Miracle and a House

I made it to forty-five years old. I was not supposed to live to be seventeen years old, and God allowed me to make it for forty-five years. Will he do it? Yes, he will do it! He did it for me. I was excited to turn forty-five years old. I was embracing my age. I do not see birthdays the way a regular person does. Yes, I am getting older, but it is a blessing. People die every day, and they do not even have a life-threatening disease, as I do.

Prior to my turning forty-five years old, my husband and I were trying to fix our credit so we could try to purchase our first home. I kept trying to rent us a home, but I was not able to get anyone to rent to me. I finally found someone willing to rent to me, but she wanted me to sign a five-year rental agreement. We were desperate and wanted out of our apartment. I was not keen on the idea of being in that lady's house for five years and paying her mortgage. I wanted to pay my own mortgage. However, once again, God blocked us from getting that woman's house, because he had a house we were going to be able to buy, not rent.

I started fixing my husband's and my credit. It took me a few months to fix both of our credit scores. Once I achieved my goal, I just needed $16,000 for a down payment to qualify for a home loan. My husband and I did not have that kind of money, and I did not know where we were supposed to get the money from. I did not have any friends or family who would loan me that kind of money, and why would I expect someone to let me borrow that amount of money? Most people did not have that kind of money.

My husband said to ask God for the money. I looked at him as if he were crazy. I said, "Do you think God is just going to hand me sixteen thousand dollars?"

He smiled and said, "He will do anything you ask him to do. Just trust him." He looked at me. "Let me ask you a question. Do you trust him?"

I looked at him and said, "Yes, I trust him."

He said, "Okay, now just ask him, and he will give you the money." I knew he was right.

One morning, I was going to a training session, and I was sitting in my car. I started praying sincerely, and I was crying. I asked God to please help me because I really needed $16,000 for a home of my own. I prayed for a while, sitting there in my car.

My little sister invited me to go to the local casino. I did not really want to go, because I was not in a good mood. However, I knew my little sister would be disappointed if I did not go, so I ended up going—and thank God I did go. I'm glad I followed my instinct and decided to go.

I met my sister and her caregiver at my sister's home. We went to my sister's favorite Chinese restaurant and ordered some food. We sat in my sister's van and ate the Chinese food. After we ate, we went to the casino.

When we got to the casino, I separated from my sister and her caregiver. I was only a few feet from them. I decided to go play a machine my friend always played when we hung out at the casino. I went to a machine, and an Asian lady was playing two separate machines. I sat in a chair next to her. I decided to play a machine on the end, near the seat I was sitting in. The Asian lady looked at me as if I were an animal or an alien. I looked back at her. She played for a little while longer. She got up and left. I decided to play one of the machines she had been playing.

I put in twenty dollars, and I won sixty dollars on top of the twenty dollars I already had, so I was up to eighty dollars. I decided to continue to play, until I got down to two dollars. My sister and her caregiver had come to stand by me while I gambled. My little sister looked at the machine and said, "You'd better stop."

I looked at her. I said, "I will." Right after I said that, I hit eighty dollars.

She said, "You'd better stop while you are ahead."

I said, "Okay, let me just play until I get to sixty dollars."

She said, "If I were you, I would stop right now."

I said, "I will stop."

I got down to sixty-eight dollars, and then I was given the opportunity to try to match three different images to win the grand prize of $16,000. I picked one. I asked my sister and her caregiver to pick one. Each of them picked one of the grand prize images, which meant I needed only one more match to win the grand prize. I was nervous so I asked my sister and her caregiver for their opinion. Turns out they thought I should pick the exact image I was already thinking about choosing. I took that as a good sign. I picked the last match, and it was the grand prize.

All the bells and whistles started ringing and going off. People started running over to my machine and bombarding me. My sister was yelling, "You won!"

I was in a state of shock. Wow, I had just won the money I needed for the down payment for my home. I won a few hundred dollars more than I needed. I won $16,828.32.

My sister said, "I'm calling your husband to tell him you won and how much you won." She called him and told him I'd won. I got on the phone and verified what she had already told him.

He said, "I told you God was going to give it to you. You just had to believe."

I said, "You were right." I told him to tell our son.

I was sitting there in my chair, when a tall black guy came and stood right behind my chair. He said, "Please do not move, ma'am." He said he was a security officer. He said, "An attendant will be here shortly. Please pull out your ID, because they will need to look at it to pay you out." He looked at the machine and said, "Wow, you won off eighty-eight cents. I just saw a white woman win one hundred fifty thousand dollars the other night, and another night, an Asian woman won two hundred fifty thousand." He smiled. "I'm glad a black woman like you finally won. A sistah finally won. Congratulations."

An attendant walked up to me, asked for my ID, took my player's card I had in the machine, and asked if I wanted my picture taken with my check or just wanted cash. I said, "I will just take the cash."

The attendant walked away, and the black security guy stayed and continued to talk with me until the attendant came back with my money. The security guard said, "I hope you don't have a small purse."

I looked at him. I held up my little purse. We both started laughing.

He said, "Every woman who wins a lot of money like you did has a small purse."

The attendant walked up to me and had me sign a form for tax purposes. She counted my money out and put the cash in my hands. I squeezed the money into my purse. The black security guard left. He came back with a white security guard. The white security guard asked if I wanted him to walk me out. I said, "Sure, that would be nice." He escorted me to my sister's van.

I was in shock. I kept thanking God for allowing me to win the money. I went home, and my husband counted it again. My son was happy. He said, "Wow, Mom, that is a lot of money." He smiled at me.

I went and put the money into the bank. I gave some money to my church. God had blessed me, after all. I kept the money in the bank for four months, until I put it down on my house.

It was a process to purchase my first home. I had a Realtor who lacked a lot of patience. He wanted me to just buy any house. However, I wanted the perfect house for me and my family. I looked at nineteen different houses before I decided to purchase the house my family and I now reside in. There were times when I wanted to give up. It was time-consuming as well as exhausting to go look for homes every day. I looked for houses the way people look for jobs. My Realtor was notorious for being late for all appointments. My son and I would end up waiting for twenty minutes for him to arrive. I was just about to give up, when I found the perfect house. I walked into the bathroom, and I fell in love with the house. It had a his-and-hers double shower and a whirlpool tub. It had a pond, a huge dog run, and an additional backyard. It had great curb appeal.

CHAPTER 23

Crisis Prevention

I turned forty-six years old last year. I had a whole lot of crises throughout the year. I usually do not get sick in the summertime, because it is typically hot. The hot weather is certainly better for my disease. However, last summer, I was working at a different jobsite, and I got sick. The two people I was working with were hot and kept turning the air conditioner on. I can't be in a cool room, because it will cause me to go into a crisis. I told them I would get sick if I got too cold. I got sick the next day. I was off work for four days.

I went back to work a week later, and they turned the air-conditioning on. Once again, I got sick. I had to monitor the air-conditioning. I had to explain to them what sickle cell was and how deadly a crisis could be.

I usually get sick in the wintertime a lot more. I ended up getting sick in October, November, and December. I had never had so many crises back-to-back like that. I was scared because the crises were frequent and bizarre. I was not used to being sick so much. However, it was wintertime, and that is when most of my crises occur. I usually try to prepare myself by making sure I dress warmly and stay as warm as I possibly can. Wintertime is the roughest season for a person with sickle cell anemia.

I also think stress plays a role with people who have sickle cell anemia. Stress can cause individuals with sickle cell anemia to go into a crisis because they are dealing with something in their lives that causes them not to feel comfortable. My life can be overwhelming due to my being married, being a mom, working, going to school, and just trying to juggle all of life's daily duties. I think sometimes I forget for a second that I have sickle cell, and I act as if I'm a regular person. I have moments when I feel so well that I forget I'm sick. I believe it is mind over matter. If you think you are sick, then you will be sick. If you keep harping on the fact that you are ill, you will feel ill. I act as if I'm well, so I stay well. My mother contributed to my being the woman I am today. She said, "You will be well as long as you speak good thoughts. You can speak things into existence." She was right. If I would have had a pity party, I would probably have died from sickle cell anemia a long time ago.

I have a hematologist, which is a doctor who keeps track of my sickle cell anemia crises. She checks my blood levels occasionally. I saw her last year after I kept getting sick. She suggested a drug that many sickle cell anemia patients are on. It is supposed to help the patient have fewer crises. She had suggested I take the medicine years ago, but I was skeptical. I decided to try it because I was having frequent crises.

I took the medicine for three weeks, and I did not do well on it at all. I was hallucinating. She'd told me prior to my taking the medicine that the worst side effect was hallucination. She'd said, "If you hallucinate, please discontinue the medicine immediately." The medicine made me feel bad. I was nauseated all the time.

She told me to keep doing what I'd been doing, because whatever I was doing was obviously working. She said, "You might have to stop going outside in extremely cold weather or weather that may be too cold for you." She typed a letter for my place of employment that said I couldn't go outside in cold or extremely hot weather. Since she wrote that letter for me, I have been a lot less sick, because I do not have to go outside in cold or extreme heat.

I'm not a psychic or anything, but I do know that if something will prevent me from going into a crisis, I will do it. I hate being sick. Crises takes a huge toll on my body.

CHAPTER 24

Writing

I am now forty-seven years old and have not had a crisis since December. I'm grateful for that. God has been good to me. However, my crises can be like earthquakes: sometimes the little crises are better than one major crisis. I'd rather have a lot of little crises than a severe crisis that causes me to be hospitalized. I hate to even go to the hospital. I try to avoid hospitals at all times. I do not even like to go visit people who are in the hospital.

I'm amazed and thankful that God gave me a gift and that I have been able to write. I started out by writing poetry when I was five years old. As I got older, I started writing raps, poetry, and short stories. When I became a young adult, I started writing fiction books. I have always had a strong passion for writing.

I wrote two books a few years ago. I wanted to publish them and even sent them to a publishing company. However, I did not have the money to pay to self-publish them. I have been sitting on my books for too many years and need to publish them. Although I wrote those books first, this book is near and dear to my heart. Sickle cell anemia is part of who I am. It played a major role in who I have become. I plan to publish my other two books later. For now, I must put all my focus on this one, because this book allows you a full picture of my life. I'm incredibly open and honest and tell you a lot about who I am. I allow you the opportunity to get up close and personal with me and how I grew up.

I felt that by telling my personal story, I could encourage as well as inspire people, whether they have sickle cell or another disease or issue they are currently coping with. I have heard other people's stories and had no direct connection to them, but I was intrigued as well as inspired by their stories, and they motivated me and gave me the strength and courage to dedicate some much-needed time to write my personal journal of my experiences with sickle cell anemia.

CHAPTER 25

Support and Encouragement

I have always been inspired by a famous singer who has sickle cell anemia. She is my role model because we have the same disease. We also have a few more things in common as well. She was a dancer, and I was a dancer. She was part of a group; I was part of several dance groups. She has one child, and I have one child. She has overcome a lot of obstacles while living with sickle cell anemia, and I have overcome many life-challenging obstacles in my life as well. I never have gotten the opportunity to see her in concert. I hope to meet her someday because we share so many things in common.

I started a sickle cell anemia group on Facebook a few years ago, but I did not get a lot of people to join the group. Most of the people in my sickle cell anemia group are my family and close friends. I was trying to reach out and solicit people who have sickle cell anemia or even know anyone with sickle cell anemia. I would like to create a platform on social media that will allow anyone who has sickle cell anemia or would like to know about it to get educated and become informed about the disease.

I would like to start a nonprofit organization for children who suffer from sickle cell anemia. I want to be a role model as well as an inspiration for people. I'm living proof that you can live a normal life with sickle cell anemia. We must be strong and know we are still able to do anything we want to do, and we must not allow sickle cell anemia to cripple us. We are stronger than most regular people because of what we have to endure.

Currently, there is no known cure for sickle cell. I hope and pray that one day there will be a cure. People always ask me, "If there was a cure, would you take it?" I say God has kept me this long, and when he is ready to take me home, I will be ready. Sickle cell is part of me, and I don't know who or what I would be if I didn't have it.

My advice to anyone who has sickle cell anemia is this: please fight like it's your last fight. Always try to stay positive, and be grateful you are alive. Don't ever be ashamed of who you are. Yes, you have a life-threatening disease, but you are a unique individual, and God chose you because he knew your strength. You know the saying "Only the strong survive." You were born with the disease and are surviving thus far, and that says a whole lot about you. It takes a special kind of person to endure the pain we have to go through during a painful crisis. My mother always told me when I was a child that I was a lot stronger than I even knew I was.

I encourage you to follow your heart and your dreams. You can do anything you want to do in this world. When I was little, I used to want to be a lawyer. I decided not to go to law school, because I didn't want to leave my mother, as I was helping her raise my little brother. I didn't even let my mother or anyone else know that I got accepted into law school in Florida. If my mama had known I got into law school, she would have insisted I go follow my dreams. I actually changed my mind and decided I wanted to be a teacher instead because I loved working with children. I went to school and got my AA degree in early childhood education. I have been working with children for almost thirty years, and I really enjoy working with them.

Go out into this world, and do whatever you want to do. Please don't allow your disease to hinder you or hold you back. You are capable of and aimed for greatness. Please share your sickle cell journey with people. Our stories are important, and we need to continue to share our personal journeys because we can educate others and bring more awareness to sickle cell anemia. The more we share our stories, the more we can let people know how serious our disease is and bring greater recognition to it. We need to make sure sickle cell anemia is known all over the world.

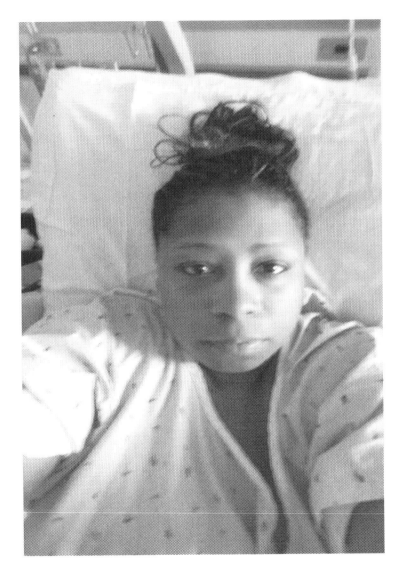

In the hospital during a sickle cell crisis

Sickle cell anemia is a horrible disease to an outsider looking in. However, to me, it is no different from any other life-threatening disease. The only difference is that sickle cell anemia does not get the much-needed recognition it deserves. People know little or nothing about the disease, because it is not seen as being as important as other well-known diseases. I have an issue with that.

I have sickle cell anemia and have been an advocate for it all my life. Sickle cell has affected me as well as many of my family members, and a lot of people in the world suffer from sickle cell anemia. Many people in the world have sickle cell anemia or know someone who has it. I decided to write my personal story because it has been quite a journey for me as a child, teenager, young adult, and middle-aged adult. I have had good days and bad days, but God has kept me, so I cannot complain.

I feel as if I have been on an emotional roller coaster of highs and then lows, and the ride will not stop. I have had some good times on this roller coaster ride and have said, "It's okay. I can ride this till the wheels fall off." God will never give any of us more than we can handle.

I have learned to weather the storm over the years. Early on, I lived according to what I expected my expiration date to be. I thought I was going to die when I was seventeen years old. I lived my life every day worried about when I was going to die, until I made it past seventeen years old. I knew it was time for me to start living each day to my full capability. I started focusing on my dreams and future goals. My life was finally worth living, and I was now living for me. I no longer allowed sickle cell anemia to control me. I was finally in control. I was surviving sickle cell anemia while trying to live a regular life.

Printed in the United States
by Baker & Taylor Publisher Services